Anonymous

A Christmas Reminder

Being the names of about eight thousand persons, a small portion of the

number confined on board the British prison ships during the war of the

revolution

Anonymous

A Christmas Reminder
*Being the names of about eight thousand persons, a small portion of the number
confined on board the British prison ships during the war of the revolution*

ISBN/EAN: 9783744789448

Printed in Europe, USA, Canada, Australia, Japan

Cover: Foto ©ninafisch / pixelio.de

More available books at **www.hansebooks.com**

A Christmas Reminder.

BEING THE NAMES OF ABOUT EIGHT THOUSAND PER-
SONS, A SMALL PORTION OF THE NUMBER
CONFINED ON BOARD THE BRITISH
PRISON SHIPS DURING THE
WAR OF THE REVO-
LUTION.

With the Compliments of the

SOCIETY OF OLD BROOKLYNITES.

Brooklyn, N. Y.:
EAGLE PRINT., 34, 36 AND 38 FULTON STREET.

1888.

Society of Old Brooklynites.

OFFICERS FOR 1887-88.

Hon. JOHN W. HUNTER, President.
EDWARD D. WHITE, First Vice-President.
ALBERT H. OSBORN, Second Vice-President.
SAMUEL A. HAYNES, Recording Secretary.
JAMES L. WATSON, M.D., Corresponding Secretary.
ALBERT H. OSBORN, Financial Secretary.
JUDAH B. VOORHEES, Treasurer.

DIRECTORS.

Hon. JOHN W. HUNTER, President, *Ex-officio.*

EDWARD D. WHITE,	ALBERT H. OSBORN,
WILLIAM H. HAZARD,	CAPT. DIEDRICH SANNEMAN,
CHARLES C. LEIGH,	JOHN WIGGINS,
JOEL SMITH,	SETH R. ROBBINS,
JOEL CONKLIN,	NICHOLAS B. RHODES,
WILLIAM E. SPRAGUE,	DANIEL T. LEVERICH,
SAMUEL A. HAYNES,	WILLIAM H. WARING,
JUDAH B. VOORHEES,	STEPHEN KIDDER,
WILLIAM M. THOMAS,	JOHN AVILA,
GEORGE W. STILLWELL,	JAMES L. WATSON, M.D.,

JOSEPH W. CAMPBELL.

STANDING COMMITTEES FOR 1887-88.

EXECUTIVE COMMITTEE.

EDWARD D. WHITE,..............88 Van Dyke street.
ALBERT H. OSBORN,.............26 Court street.
JUDAH B. VOORHEES,...........Surrogate's Office, Hall of Records.
CHARLES C. LEIGH,..............4 Willow street.
S. WARREN SNEDEN,............131 Prospect Place.

FINANCE COMMITTEE.

DANIEL T. LEVERICH,.... .....76 Hicks street.
CAPT. DIEDRICH SANNEMAN,.. .52 Hicks street.
GEORGE W. STILLWELL,........211 Thirteenth street.

COMMITTEE ON MEMBERSHIP.

JOHN W. WIGGINS,.... ....377 Gold street.
WILLIAM E. SPRAGUE,.......... 456 Adelphi street.
JOEL CONKLIN,............... 396 Bridge street.

COMMITTEE ON HISTORY, ARTS AND SCIENCES.

ALBERT H. OSBORN,.............26 Court street.
JAMES L. WATSON, M.D.,........9 Elm Place.
STEPHEN KIDDER,........ ......138 Atlantic street.
CHARLES C. LEIGH,........ .....4 Willow street.
WILLIAM M. THOMAS,.......... 219 Schermerhorn street.

The Society of Old Brooklynites take great pleasure in presenting to you the names of eight thousand of the prisoners who were confined on board the British prison ship "Jersey" during a part of the Revolutionary war.

After diligent research among the records of the British War Department, access to which was kindly permitted by Her Majesty's Government, this is all that can be found ; and these are from the records of this one ship only. No record of the names of any of the prisoners of the prison ships "Scorpion," "John," "Strombolo," "Falmouth," "Hunter," "Prince of Wales" and "Transport" can be found ; though their log-books make very frequent mention of prisoners having been received on board. The list here presented is therefore but a small portion of those of our fellow citizens who were confined on board those floating Golgothas. Nor is it possible to designate which of these names died on board, but authentic history, within the memory of the parents of many now living, proves that the number that died and were buried on our shores, and over whose remains we now desire to erect a monument worthy of these patriots, numbered more than twelve thousand.

From these floating dungeons, the hearts of whose keepers must have delighted in the luxury of woe, the bodies of our countrymen after death were taken on shore, and one of our Revolutionary poets thus describes the manner in which their remains were disposed of :

> "Each day at least six carcasses we bore,
> And scratched their graves along the sandy shore ;
> By feeble hands the shallow graves were made.
> No stone memorial o'er the corpses laid ;
> In barren sands and far from home they lie.
> No friend to shed a tear when passing by ;
> O'er the mean tombs insulting Britons tread.
> Spurn at the sand and curse the rebel dead."

This Society, numbering between two and three hundred members, who must have resided in the city at least fifty years before being eligible to membership, have at great expense procured these names, and they have also caused plans and specifications of a proposed monument to the memory of these departed patriots to be prepared and forwarded to Congress, and procured the signatures of about twenty thousand citizens to the accompanying petition asking the Congress of the United States to erect the same over their remains.

The efforts of the Society in this direction have met the universal approbation of the people and of the press of the country. The Board of Supervisors of Kings County, the Board of Aldermen of the City of New York and the Legislature of the State of New York, have all passed resolutions, copies of which are printed herewith, commending the project and requesting Congress to grant the petition of the Society.

The bones of these martyrs lie interred in a permanent tomb in this city, but without a mark of any kind to inform the stranger as to the nature and object of the structure, and it is the earnest desire of this Society to remedy this defect, and to endeavor to do tardy justice to the memory of those to whose firmness and patriotism we owe our liberties and the blessings of the good government we enjoy.

To the Senate and House of Representatives of the United States, in Congress assembled :

Your petitioners, an incorporated society of the City of Brooklyn, under the title of the " SOCIETY OF OLD BROOKLYN-ITES," would respectfully represent :

That the remains of more than 12,000 martyrs to the cause of liberty lie entombed in this city, who died during our Revolutionary war on board the prison ships of the British at the Wallabout, and which were buried on our shores during that memorable struggle, many of which were by the action of the waves washed out of their shallow graves,—their bones scattered along the beach, exposed to the Summer's sun and Winter's storms, until the year 1808, when the Tammany Society or Columbian Order, of the City of New York, had them collected and buried with imposing ceremonies, in which the governors of several States, mayors of cities, and civil, military and ecclesiastical dignitaries from all parts of the country took part.

The place of burial was on Jackson street, in this city, and the tomb, a temporary wooden structure, in which they were placed, became so dilipidated by reason of changes made in the surroundings and from natural decay, that the sacred remains were again exposed to the gaze of the multitude, until the Park Commissioners of this city, with the sanction of the city government, prepared with great care and expense a permanent and imperishable tomb for their reception on the historic ground of Fort Greene, a charming elevation in Washington Park, in this city, overlooking the scene of their sufferings and death—to which the sacred remains were carefully removed and deposited.

Those devoted patriots, from every one of the original thirteen States, were prisoners of war, taken by the British army and navy, and numbered more than were killed in all the battles, both by sea and land, in that long and desperate struggle for freedom.

When it is remembered that constant and unremitting efforts were made by the British officers to induce these prisoners to purchase their freedom and save their lives by enlisting in the service of the enemy; that many, probably the majority of them, had families who were suffering by reason of their absence ; that to remain in these horrible prisons was almost certain death, and that under all these circumstances they remained faithful to the cause in which they had enlisted and preferred death to dishonor ; we must concede that they earned the title of "MARTYRS OF THE PRISON SHIPS," and deserve such recognition from the Government, to aid in the establishment of which they sacrificed their lives, as will show to the world that republics are not ungrateful, but that we cherish their memories, honor their devotion to their country, and will erect such an enduring monument to commemorate their virtues as will stimulate future generations to emulate their patriotism.

We therefore most respectfully ask that your honorable body will make an appropriation of not less than one hundred thousand dollars toward the erection of a suitable monument, to be erected at or near the spot where their sacred remains now lie, the site for which will be donated for that purpose by the City of Brooklyn.

This society will most cheerfully give all the aid in their power toward the accomplishment of the object of this Petition.

Very respectfully,

JOHN W. HUNTER, *President.*

SAML. A. HAYNES, *Secretary.*

BROOKLYN, January 5th, 1888.

Concurrent resolutions relative to erecting a monument to the Martyrs of the British ships at the Wallabout during the Revolutionary war :

STATE OF NEW YORK,
IN SENATE, ALBANY, Feb. 28, 1888.

Whereas, the Society of Old Brooklynites of the City of Brooklyn has presented a petition to the Congress of the United States for the erection of a monument to commemorate the virtues and patriotism of more than twelve thousand soldiers and sailors, who perished on board the prison ships at the Wallabout during the Revolutionary war, and

Whereas, these unhappy victims were citizens of the United States, prisoners of war, captured while in the service of this country during its long and desperate struggle for freedom when the Government was too feeble to afford them protection or relieve their sufferings ; therefore,

Resolved, if the Assembly concur, that the Senators and Representatives in Congress from this State be, and they hereby are earnestly requested to use all honorable means in their power to secure the passage of the bill (H. R. 18,877), having for its object the erection of a monument to the memory of the martyrs of the prison ships.

Resolved, if the Assembly concur, that a duly certified copy of the foregoing preamble and resolution be forwarded to each Senator and Representative in Congress from this State.

By order,

JOHN S. KENYON,
Clerk.

IN ASSEMBLY, Feb. 28, 1888.

Concurred in without amendment.

By order of the Assembly,

C. H. CHICKERING,
Clerk.

The following was adopted unanimously by the Common Council of the City of New York :

Whereas, the Society of Old Brooklynites, of the City of Brooklyn, has presented a petition to the Congress of the United States for the erection of a monument on Fort Greene, in said city, to commemorate the virtues of those martyrs of the cause of liberty who died on board the prison ships at the Wallabout during the war of the Revolution ; and

Whereas, it is the opinion of this Common Council that it is the duty of Congress to fitly commemorate the manly virtues and stern patriotism of more than twelve thousand citizens of the United States who, when prisoners of war, refused to purchase their lives by enlisting in the service of the enemy and preferred death to dishonor ; therefore

Resolved, that this Common Council heartily endorse the patriotic efforts of the Society of Old Brooklynites, and earnestly request the members of Congress from this city to favor, by all honorable means in their power, the passage of the bill now pending for the erection of the proposed monument in honor of the martyrs of the prison ships.

Resolved, that a certified copy of the foregoing preamble and resolutions under the seal of the City be forwarded to every member of Congress from this city.

Kings County Board of Supervisors, }
Brooklyn, Jan. 24, 1888. }

Adopted the following :

Whereas, the Society of Old Brooklynites of the City of Brooklyn have petitioned the Congress of the United States for an appropriation to fitly commemorate by a monument the martyrs of the prison ships of the Revolutionary war, and

Whereas, this Board heartily approves of the motives and patriotic zeal of the said society in the noble effort to inspire devotion to country, perpetuating the virtues of those who sacrificed their lives for republican principles, thus stimulating future generations to emulate their patriotism, therefore be it

Resolved, that we most cordially extend to the Society of Old Brooklynites our earnest support and encouragement, and express the hope that their efforts will be rewarded by the people through their representatives in Congress.

At a very large meeting of soldiers and citizens held on Sunday May 27, 1888, at the Tomb of the Martyrs, on Fort Greene, in honor of the heroes who perished on board the prison ships, after singing by the children of the public schools and religious services, and an eloquent address by one of the generals of the late war, the following were unanimously adopted :

Whereas, the Society of Old Brooklynites has petitioned Congress for an appropriation of one hundred thousand dollars for the erection of a monument to the memory of those we are here assembled to honor ; therefore,

Resolved, that Congress are hereby earnestly requested to pass the bill presented by the Hon. Felix Campbell for that object, believing that no more worthy object can claim the attention of Congress than thus to honor the memory of that gallant army, who, when persistently importuned to choose between the prison ships and enlistment in the army of the king, exclaimed *"give us the prison ships and death, or Washington and liberty!"*

Resolved, that such a monument is necessary to preserve the spirit of patriotism that imbued the founders of this Republic from the accumulating influence of wealth and luxury and to teach future generations that the Republic is not ungrateful but that we honor their virtues and will commemorate their glorious deeds in imperishable granite.

Resolved, that this preamble and resolutions be signed by the officers of the meeting and transmitted to each member of Congress.

> JOHN W. HUNTER, Chairman.
> THOMAS RULAN, Commander.
> WILLIAM A. POWERS, G. A. R., Kings Co.

We, the undersigned, a Committee appointed by the Society of Old Brooklynites, to place in alphabetical order the following names, certify we have performed this with great care and they are a faithful copy of the original. And we further entreat the reader from whatever part of our country you live to make a copy of the petition of our society and have it signed by your neighbors, wives and children, and send it to Congress. for you are as much interested as yours very respectfully,

> DANIEL T. LEVERICH.
> CHAS. C. LEIGH.
> DIEDRICH SANNEMAN.
> FREDERICK J. HOSFORD.

PRISONERS CONFINED ON BOARD THE BRITISH SHIP "JERSEY."

Alexander, Lehle
Adams, Warren
Anthony, Davis
Anthony, Lemuel
Arnold, David
Augusta, Peter
Avery, Job
Allison, Robert
Alexander, John
Atkins, Silas
Allen, John
Abbett, John
Andrews, Pasquitt
Anrandes, Joseph.
Allegree, Francis
Aleslure, Jean
Antonf, Francis
Attera, Duke
Atlin, James
Allen, John
Ashburn, John
Allen, William
Audit, Joseph
Adams, Moses
Allen, Richard
Allen, Bucknell
Alden, Humphrey
Adams, Joseph
Augustine, Thomas
Arme, Esikiel
Andrews, John
Allen, Thomas
Adams, John
Antone, Jean
Aston, Edward
Allen, Benjamin
Anderson, David
Adams, Pisco
Almon, Arrohan
Andrews, Pisco
Anderson, John
Andrews, Thomas
Anderson, William
Alignott, George
Albion, Robert

Allen, Isaac
Aldridge, George
Atkinson, William
Armstrong, William
Arcos, Thomas
Allen, William
Atkins, John
Allison, Brady
Aquirse, Joseph
Allen, John
Ashley, John
Alexander, Archibald
Ash, Henry
Allen, William
Antonio, John
Atham, John
Askin, John
Askin, John
Atwood, Samuel
Adams, Isaac
Adams, Amos
Allison, Bradby
Adams, Lawrence
Alexander, John
Allen, Backnel
Anthony, David
Abbott, John
Adams, John
Allis, Caleb
Andrews, Pascal
Anton, Jean
Antiqua, Jaque
Addams, Amos
Addison, Benjamin
Allan, Gideon
Adams, John
Adams, David
Allen, Samuel
Aston, Thomas
Anderson, William
Annapolen, Andre D. C.
Allen, Richard
Americk, Peter
Angell, James
Ashbury, Benjamin

Armsby, Elijah
Abois, Christopher
Addett, John
Anderson, William
Appleton, Samuel
Aitken, Robert
Andrews, John
Allen, Squire
Adams, Nathaniel
Armsed, Jean
Andre, Jean
Alment, Frances
Angola, Dominique
Adams, Stephen
Arnolds, Samuel
Avmev, Benjamin
Amnell, Henry
Anderson, Robert
Armstrong, Christian
Anthony, Samuel
Andrews, Benjamin
Alvertson, Thomas
Allan, Hugh
Anderson, William
Atkinson, John
Allan, John
Alsworth, James
Admister, Noah
Admistad, Robert
Alsfrugh, Jacob
Adlott, John
Alstright, Jacob
Andrews, John
Allen, Samuel
Adams, Benjamin
Abing, Philip
Allen, Samuel
Adams, Benjamin
Anderson, Charles
Aldkin, Frederick
Aberry, Jacob
Alwood, George
Andrews, John
Archer, John
Ancette, Jean

Augillia, Anthony
Andrews, Ebeneser
Allen, Josiah
Allen, Thomas
Allin, Jean
Allen, Samuel
Andre, George
Andrews, Thomas
Allen, Bancke
Andrews, Frances
Argause, Frances
Alexander, William
Andrie, Guillion
Abington, Thomas
Alwood, James
Alpin, William
Aguyneble, Thomas
Arnolds, Charles
Albert, Piere
Albert, Charles
Andrews, William
Abrams, Daniel
Aires, John
Akens, Jacob
Anderson, Thomas
Aenbie, Jean
Antien, Peire
Aliev, Joseph
Aliet, Christopher
Arnabald, Samuel
Alwhite, James
Anster, William
Arnold, Amos
Affille, Frances
Auchinlaup, Henry
Allen, Ebeneser
Archer, Abraham
Andrews, Frederick
Ash, James
Aboms, William
Aujet, Laurie
Addon, David
Ashley, Warren
Allison, James
Aessinis, Michael
Ajote, Manuel
Aspuro, Frances
Anaza, Austin
Anson, John
Amingo, Anthony

Aaron, John
Aarons, Garret
Adovie, James
Aaron, John
Adams, Thomas
Appell, Daniel
Allen, William
Azoala, Don Pedro
Acito, Gansio
Armutage, James
Amey, Charles
Arraz, ———
Arnold, Samuel
Andrews, Jerediah
Armold, Benjamin
Allen, George
Ashby, John
Ashby, Warren
Atwood, John
Ashbey John
Adams, Thomas
Able, George
Ariel, Richard
Arnold, Ash
Anabal, Nathaniel
Abel, Abel
Apple, Daniel
Augusion, Igarz Babu
Abusure, Don Meegl
Aldarouda, Pedro
Arismane, Asencid
Aedora, Sebastion de
Alcorta, Joseph De
Artall, Man'l de
Alcorta, Juan Ignacid
Aguirra, Joseph Antonio
Amizarma, Man'l
Arral, Andres
Arreche, Joseph
Alconam, Joachin
Alvarey, Thomas
Alverd, Don Ambrose
Asevasuo, Don Pedro
Aiz, Thomas
Alveras, Miguel
Asevlado, Hosea
Allan, Thomas
Ashton, John
Alchipike, Jacob
Ashto, Thomas

Anderson, Simon
Anderson, W
Atkins, George
Arnold, Thomas
Allen, Murgo
Allen, Samuel
Adamson, William
Askill, Andrew
Archer, James
Aker, Joseph
Adebon, John
Adamson, William
Alsough, Jacob
Ash, Henry
Alvey, Joseph
Adams, John
Ashburn, Peter
Adams, Abel
Andrews, Anthony
Arbay, ———
Allah, Joseph
Adamson, William
Aker, Joseph
Archer, Stephen
Abben, James
Andrews, Jonathan
Ayrse, Frances
Andrews, Dollar
Atkinson, Robert
Ause, Piere
Atton, Jean Piere
Adams, Richard
Allen, Samuel
Appleby, Thomas
Abbett, Alexander
Andrie, Pashell
Allen, Samuel
Alden, Humphrey
Abett, Jabes
Austin, George
Allen, Gideon
Anthony, John
Almond, Aceth
Antonio, John
Andrews, Philany
Attwell, John
Allen, John
Allen, John
Alger, Thomas
A. Hasen Nathaniel

Akerson, Richard	Brice, John	Brooks, Samuel
Adams, Abel	Bunker, William	Blunt, George
Anderson, Joseph	Baker, Nathaniel	Brene, Piere
Abbott, Daniel	Boker, Reuben	Brere, Joseph
Brooks, Charles	Baxter, Molaqa	Baptisto, Jean
Burke, William	Butler, John	Backalong, Antonio
Bill, John	Bridges, Thomas	Brown, Joseph
Barnes, Wood	Black, James	Bishop, Ezekiel
Blair, John	Bowers, James	Blodget, Seth
Beal, Samuel	Bryon, Berry	Benjamin, Iman
Blayner, Asa	Berry, William	Bucklin, Daniel
Bavedon, Benjamin	Bucklin, Daniel	Butler, Abner
Butler, Paul	Bill, Charles	Brown, William
Bowman, Elijah	Baker, Judah	Baker, Christopher
Butlolph, George	Broad, Ephraim	Bullock, Benjamin
Beaufort, Joseph	Blunt, George	Bullock, Thomas
Burnett, James	Bunker, William	Bayley, John
Briton, Peter	Blodget, Juan	Blanchet, William
Blaekhunt, Alexander	Bason, William	Bocrous, Jonathan
Beebe, Daniel	Brooks, Thomas	Broad, Ephraim
Bobier, John	Brown, John	Burkman, Michael
Bradford, Pelig	Bryant, James	Barns, Wooding
Bradford, John	Barton, Thomas	Burries, Jonathan
Burnett, Piere	Brire, Louis	Batchelor, Asa
Bate, Benjamin	Bachelier, Francis	Bodin, Lewis
Bullock, Benjamin	Bosse, Jaque	Billings, Esekiel
Bently, Nathaniel	Boyer, Francis	Billows, David
Bransdale, William	Bandine, Piere	Black, James
Bartly, Joseph	Boiron, Pierre	Beard, Moses
Braily, Nathaniel	Boyer, Jaque	Boen, Martin
Buddington, Jonathan	Brown, Jonathan	Bishop, John
Burdett, John	Brown, Peter	Burnett, James
Billings, Benjamin	Bounett, Piere	Bagley, Adam
Bogat, Roper	Boelourne, John	Bartley, Joseph
Billings, Bradford	Bodwayne, Peter	Black, John
Buddington, Walter	Bowes, Fulbum	Bishop, John
Benton, David	Blambo, Gideon	Boneafoy, Jeremiah
Barnes, Henry	Banaby, Peter	Brown, William
Blayner, Asa	Brown, Thomas	Bonus, Barnabus
Blanch, Robert	Bell, Robert	Brown, Gustavus
Beekman, James	Batchelor, Asa	Barney, Henry
Bramber, William	Blaque, Jesse	Bierd, David
Buckley, Francis	Briton, Jalaher C.	Bierd, Charles
Blevin, Edward	Brownwell, Charles	Black, Joseph
Barnett, Cyptra	Brownwell, Gardner	Bell, Aaron
Baily, William	Bailey, Samuel	Blond, John
Babcock, William	Boggart, James	Braden, William
Berry, John	Brown, Francis	Bunce, Lewis
Burroughs, John	Brown, John	Blake, Increase
Bud, Benjamin	Baker, Pembleton	Berryman, William

Bamper, Jacob	Boswell, Gustavus	Boulding. Theopolis
Beebe, Joshua	Burnhill, Thomas	Brown, Hugh
Brown, John	Briggs, John	Bell, Charles
Blanney, John	Baker, John	Bachelor, Asa
Beal, Daniel	Butler, James	Babcock, Franklin
Berry, Simon	Black, Samuel	Bill, Garden
Barnhouse, William	Brown, James	Bedell, Frances
Bruster, Joseph	Boswell, Gustavus	Butler, James
Burdit, Daniel	Bazee, John	Barsidge, Francis
Bradford, John	Bryan, John	Berrycruise, Philip
Briggs, William	Bloome, Peter	Baker, Ebeneser
Bussy, Nathaniel	Bonauf, Haloran	Barker, Benjamin
Baison, William	Beard, Robert	Bennett, Elisha
Brand, James	Blumbarg, George	Barker, Jacom
Burr, Stephen	Bloome, Peter	Bacon, Juda
Bryer, Joseph	Black, Philip	Bacon, Benjamin
Bennett, Piere	Belcher, Joseph	Berry, Benjamin
Berry, William	Broddin, Lewis	Berry, Peter
Barrett, William	Black, James	Bowman, Daniel
Bengier, Jean	Bailey, William	Buek, John
Bonifiri, Antony	Butler, William	Burton, James
Boding, Louis	Berry, William	Bunker, Timothy
Bolong, Jean	Blunt, George	Burden, Jeremiah
Bonesca, Jean	Baker, Pamberton	Brush, Asron
Blong, Louis	Brooks, Aaron	Blaisdell, William
Bercont, Francis	Bryan, John	Bolton, John
Bouting, Jean	Burrage, Francis	Briek, Thadeus
Bonfier, Pierre	Brown, Merrit	Burch, Thomas
Bucklin, Daniel	Brown, Thomas	Browne, William
Bissell, John	Barkump, Joseph	Benloyde, Joseph
Blinde, Joseph	Brade, Jessee	Biola, Cirretto
Brown, Willis	Bayess, Thomas	Brisque, Domingo
Bearde, Moses	Bates, Benjamin	Bedford, Thomas
Banks, Mathew	Buckwith, Samuel	Bartlett, William
Buckley, Jacob	Buckwith, Thomas	Buneh, Thomas
Burdock, Vincent	Bowles, James	Biran, Piere
Beatty, Daniel	Baker, Pemberton	Buchanan, Frances
Borus, Daniel, 2	Bryan, Isar	Bousgee, Athanase
Boven, Edward	Bryan, John	Burwell, Ivan
Barnhouse, William	Baird, Moses	Bertain, Martin
Buck, Elias	Baekay, Francis	Byanslo, Jessee
Brown, James	Bourslie, Laurence	Bigalo, Benjamin
Brovert, John	Boursbo, John	Birmingham, Samuel
Buck, Elisha	Boen, Esekiel	Barley, John
Braden, William	Brown, David	Bapbsta, Rio John
Bailey, Thomas	Butter, James	Bluff, Havming
Braden, James	Bibbistone, Robert	Boase, Augustus
Bagger, John	Burn, William	Belgran, Piere
Broderic, Richard	Boswell, Ebeneser	Blossom, Peter
Brown, John	Bravney, Whitton	Buddington, Oliver

Bone, Henry
Bailey, John
Badeno, Laurence
Bright, Alexander
Blowden, William
Bearbank, James
Banks, John
Barber, Gilbert
Blake, James
Barker, John
Bristo, Simon
Blake, Valentine
Buckworth, David
Badiek, William
Boar, Mathew
Black, Samuel
Baumnos,——
Bentley, Nathaniel
Boen, Purden
Brown, William
Bueklein, Joseph
Butts, Benjamin
Billing, Samuel
Buckley, Daniel
Brewer, John
Bird, Weldon
Beszick, John
Barney, Mons
Babier, Jean
Bartleine, Petrus
Broge, Joseph
Branel, Charles
Belding, John
Bowen, Pardon
Bacon, George
Branch, Alolibah
Brayton, Burdon
Brayton, Peter
Bishop, Israel
Burden, William
Brown, Benjamin
Bylight, John
Braswan, Peter
Brown, Samuel
Bachelor, Jonathan
Bradbridge, Thomas
Baisalus, Joseph
Bernall, Lewis
Brewett, Joseph
Bowscas, Jean

Buas, Simon
Bernadus, Frances
Branard, James
Branard, Stephen
Brewster, Seabury
Brown, John
Ball, Thomas
Berry, Alexander
Brown, William
Black, Robert N.
Booth, John
Bryan, Nathaniel
Brown, W
Baston, Louis
Baldwin, Ralph
Bassett, W
Burns, Archibald
Brader, James
Bamford, Ralf
Bushell, James
Bragley, William
Bradford, Joseph
Butler Francis
Bailey, John
Bacon, Esau
Boen, Christopher
Barry, Samuel
Bryan, William
Bowen, Willis
Beck, Thomas
Britton, Thomas
Brocton, Joshua
Bowman, John
Batt, William
Biglow, Joseph
Burnett, Frederick
Burra, Piere
Bartholomew, Charles
Bonea, Anthony
Bouea, Anthony
Boudet, Augustin
Brown, John
Burns, John
Brown, James
Barnhill, Thomas
Berger, Julian
Bottis, Charles
Bussong, Piere
Boiad, Nicholas
Beckwith, Walter

Bill, John
Burke, James
Bearbank, William
Bryant, Benjamin
Bryant, Ephraim
Butterman, George
Brown, William
Baldwin, Nathaniel
Baldwin, David
Bunwell, Frederick
Bradford, Amos
Broadly, Ossia
Bradly, Abijah
Bradly, Alijah
Busler, Elisha
Barker, Peter
Blately, Joseph
Burgh, Barnard
Brehard, James
Barnell, Ethiem
Bowrge, Lewis
Bortuslies, Joseph
Baptist, Jean
Barracks, James
Benn, John
Bushall, James
Bouton, Lewis
Buckley, Jacob
Belcher, John
Blake, Samuel
Brown, Thomas
Bunke, Obadiah
Bartol, Michael
Bradon, James
Black, Isaac
Burnhill, Thomas
Burnhill, Daniel
Berry, Thesdra
Bradley, James
Brownhill, Wanton
Brownhill, Essick
Banker, James
Buckley, Cornelius
Blackburn, John
Bagges, Barnett
Brown, John
Buchen, Thomas
Butler, James
Bryon, Thomas
Bitton, Peter

14

Baptist, Gale	Branson, David	Bill, Charles
Baxula, Jean	Brooks, Henry	Bolt, William
Biller, James	Battersby, John	Begonies, Jean
Birket, Thomas	Butler, John	Bertine, Jean
Barre, Abner	Blythe, William	Brown, John
Bollier, Jaques	Balding, James	Bryan, Edward
Burhan, Jean	Bissick, Jack	Boutilla, Jean
Brooks, Samuel	Bass, Dounor	Baldwin, William
Batton, John	Blacpond, John	Baker, Thomas
Brown, Joseph	Bandel, James	Bray, Robert
Babell, Jeremiah	Biskney, Anthony	Burnett, Joseph
Bliss, William	Barba, John	Binnen, Frarey
Bobham, Joseph	Brown, Patrick	Bilarie, Jean
Blevin, Evan	Berry, John	Boyean, David
Bradford, Peleg	Bowdon, Elijah	Brown, Christopher
Black William	Berry, Daniel	Brown, Hugh
Brown, Gustavus	Besen, Andrew	Bowen, Elijah
Bloomfield James	Banister, John	Barden, John
Bradfield, Samuel	Bludget, John	Bowen, William
Barnes, Charles	Budica, John	Beckford, Benjamin
Burgess, Henry	Buckley, Jacob	Bradford, William
Bosiere, Piere	Barrett, Enoch	Brown, Michael
Butler, John	Bradley, Daniel	Bumbley, Benjamin
Bunting, Merdock	Brewster, James	Baker, Thomas
Bushard, John	Boyne, Joseph	Budgid, William
Barrett, Francis	Benson, Anthony	Bussause, Nicholas
Brows, Piere	Brown, Foggs William	Bennett, Peter
Bruton, Daniel	Boney, James	Bray, Robert
Baxter, George	Banks, William	Barney, Samuel
Bransdale, William	Burd, Michael	Bowree, John
Butler, John	Bentley, William	Barber, John
Barkly, Benjamin	Brim, Henry	Berry, Edward
Bowen, Arden	Blissfield, Samuel	Barret, Samuel
Bain, George	Butler, John	Brun, Lewis
Blake, Charles	Brown, John	Brown, John
Bryant, William	Battesker, John	Bortley, Joseph
Beebe, Benjamin	Bowers, Thomas	Beaumont, Pirri
Bedford, Joseph	Buckley, John	Boutempt, Jean
Bark, Mabas	Bargeman, Walter	Bass, Thomas
Bissole, Osee	Burriss, Nathaniel	Birch, Nathaniel
Busk, Miles	Bates, Henry	Billings, William
Ballard, Benjamin	Bentley, Peter	Buldings, John
Brown, David	Bell, Uriah	Bottom, James
Boyle, John	Bill, Pierre	Bottom, Walter
Boyd, William	Burton, John	Bunce, Norman
Boyd, Thomas	Bedford, Frederick	Burnham James
Bartholomew, Joseph	Brown, Samuel	Brown, Joseph
Boyde, John	Blancher, Joseph	Bools, Thomas
Barrett, Dennis	Borrell, James	Brown, Christopher
Bloomfield, Samuel	Baker, Lemuel	Billows, Asa

Bennett, John	Branton, John	Bice, John
Billard, Jean	Beldarraiun, Elarado	Baptista, Juan
Bevin, Jean	Bandeie, Augustin	Berra, Juan Juquacid
Bretton, Piere	Barthalemerd, Charles	Borda, Joseph
Bargo, Charles	Bund, Antuno	Berasan, Josh M.
Burgo, Posper	Berner, Pierre	Balumatigua, Joseph
Bulgedo, Jonathan	Bormen, John	Bradbury, Samuel
Bausto, Thomas	Begand, Lewis	Bitgayse, Piere
Black, John	Brandford, Ralf *	Bonamie, Augustine
Baldin, Thomas	Bickety, John	Bryean, Frances
Biggs, Thomas	Bowen, Thomas	Byard, Nicholas
Blanch, David	Bussong, Peter	Babtreause, Vascilla,
Butler, Robert	Bearbank, Jesse	Bertram, John
Bolts, William	Babel, James	Blossom, James
Bentler, Peter	Brooks, Paul	Bowman, Benjamin
Batterman, George	Brenward, Elijah	Bastine, Michael
Batterman, Adar	Books, William	Bennett, George
Billings, Robert	Blaynald, Lubal	Burrell, Lewis
Bevcloa, Samuel	Baker, John	Bragg, Ebeneser
Bunson, Richard	Beckett, William	Borden, Charles
Bowers, James	Beckwith, Jonathan	Brown, John
Bosey, ——	Boine, William	Bowner, Michael
Buffoot, Laurence	Benton, John	Barker, Thomas
Bong, Thomas	Boudery, Augustus	Bartholoyd, Benjamin
Bond, Joseph	Beck, Andrew	Baston, Richard
Bartholomew ——	Brinkley, Peter	Bluard, William
Baynes, Joseph	Boyd, John	Baddock, Jonathan
Bayde, Joseph	Brown, Nathaniel	Brown, James
Baker, Joseph	Butler, James	Byson, Charles
Baker, Thomas	Bloxand, John	Broarker, Joseph
Beard, Morgan	Beebe, Elias	Brion, Ephraim
Brewer, Samuel	Bescroft, William	Burgess, Theopolis
Baboard, Abel	Brent, George	Bussman, William
Bogle, Ralph	Bellard, Alexander	Burk, Thomas
Byrnes, Hugh	Bevan, Samuel	Bodham, Robert
Boyd, James	Brown, Jacob	Barroll, Robert
Bimbley, Benjamin	Black, Timothy	Baron, Barnard
Buckler, Philip	Black, Daniel	Badante, Stephen
Berry, Benjamin	Bates, James	Bargeron, Joseph
Brent, George	Barman, James	Barrett, Piere
Basker, John	Batterman, Joseph	Buger, John
Bett, James	Bigelow, Oliver	Brown, John
Benham, Joseph	Brainard, Zachcus	Buson, Garde
Bunce, Norman	Burdock, Robert	Bowrie, P. I.
Baldwin, John	Burdock, Bleck	Bonovist, Bartholomew
Beshire, Jean	Brainer, Zachery	Bertine, Perri
Blone, Lewis	Brainer, Joseph	Blaine, V. C.
Blowen, John	Bugg, Silas	Bird, Joseph
Barenoft, William	Benson, Stizer	Bragg, Ebenezer
Barret, Charles	Brown, Samuel	Byise, Bortholomew

Bennet, Joseph
Budd, Nicholas
Barrot, Enoch
Berry, Dennis
Beck, Andrew
Brown, James
Bartholomew, William
Bush, Stephen
Bartow, Andrew
Brand, William
Burrow, Edward
Batterman, George
Batterman, Adam
Black, Charles
Bradly, Abraham,
Barton, William
Briggs, Caleb
Brooker, William
Bick, Andrew
Bryan, Mathew
Bamfora, Ralf,
Bartow, Josiah
Bruding, James
Boyan, John
Briger, Gloud
Belugh, Julian
Belter, Joseph
Beane, Joseph
Broderick, William
Berean, Joseph
Butler, John
Burdis, Jasan
Burrester, Isaac
Berry, Abner
Buckley, Daniel
Bryen, Richard
Burney, James
Bales, Thomas
Baitho, William
Brown, Hugh
Bell, Charles
Burns, Henry
Bleven, Henry
Butcher, William
Brown, George
Butler, Daniel
Barnett, John
Bayan, Richard
Burrell, John
Beankey, James

Bank, Mathew
Beard, Moses
Bennett, John
Bousetter, John
Bartlett, James
Begley, Joseph
Bennet, John
Brown, Willis
Burns, Archibald
Bobgea, John
Brewster, James
Broderick, William
Burder, Joseph
Beasell, Benjamin
Blunt, George
Bothal, Lewis
Bowden, Abijah
Bartlett, Jonathan
Ballast, John
Broderic, Philip
Barker, Edward
Bahamony, Joseph
Bunker, Jonathan
Bush, Myles
Barbein, Ebeneser
Burns, Edward
Brisk, Thomas
Banister, John
Brady, John
Bryan, John
Birch, Alexander
Buffins, Joshua
Beverly, Benjamin
Brooks, Charles
Bredford, John
Bastin, Juvery
Bievey, Joshua
Brown, John
Coffin, Richard
Chase, Augustus
Chase, Earl
Cariviot, Joseph
Carender, Joseph
Case, Nathaniel
Canama, Joseph
Chevalier, Jean
Cajole, Piere
Crusanews, Joseph
Clabe, Piere
Cavalier, Francis

Comone, Jaque
Comone, Bartholomew
Cruse, John Antony
Cavensa, Gasinto
Carney, Anthony
Cownovan, Edward
Cobbs, Raymond
Carret, Piere
Clerk, John
Cheesbrook, David
Cheesbrook, Samuel
Chase, George
Clerk, Gambeton
Crawford, William
Charles, James
Colam, David
Cain, David
Cannon, Joseph
Collins, Joseph
Crawford, Benjamin
Clerk, Thomas
Combs, John
Collins, John
Colley, Basquite
Copeland, Joseph
Combs, John
Coleman, David
Crawford, John
Chappell, Charles
Cox, William
Clire, Philip
Christie, James
Colville, David
Cressouson, Henry
Chamberlin, Benjamin
Cadat, Louis
Crowell, Bissell
Cox, Joseph
Craft, Mathias
Cole, Benjamin
Church, Benjamin
Cromwell, Oliver
Cook, Ezekiel
Cooper, Mathew
Chase, Aaron
Carter, George
Champney, Benjamin
Coop, Ezekiel
Cocklin, John
Crosby, Daniel

Crocker, Benjamin
Caddock, Natham
Calman, Andrew
Clerk, Andrew
Cotton, William
Collins, Powell
Cook, Eashek
Carrow, John
Cawrier, John
Collins, John
Carr, Edward
Caransame, William
Cromwell, Oliver
Carey, John
Cox, John
Clerk, John
Cook, Richard
Crayton, Isaac
Cullen, William
Carson, William
Caswell, John
Conner, James
Cadet, Louis
Cooper, Mott
Crane, Philip
Crane, Samuel
Coughin, John
Casey, Richard
Crispin, William
Cain, David
Chase, Aaron
Cunningham, Barnabus
Colwell, Nathaniel
Clerk, Nathaniel
Carroll, Michael
Chaplin, Joseph
Chaplin, Josiah
Cromwell, Oliver
Champny, Benjamin
Crowell, Bissell
Carroll, James
Cox, Enoch
Clannon, Benjamin
Chevalier, Benjamin
Cumstock, Cornelius
Chapman, John
Culbert, Daniel
Chamberlain, Benjamin
Cox, Jacob
Clay, John

Collins, William
Chappell, Frederick
Chamberlain, Charles
Cooper, Nathaniel
Crape, Abraham
Culbarth, Thomas
Chamrell, Job
Callchan, William
Carr, William
Croppen, John
Cloud, John
Capnell, Daniel
Conner, William
Carns, Davis
Casey, William
Convass, William
Charles, John
Case, Peter
Cooper, Richard
Campbell, Joseph
Cheesbrook, Pierre
Cheesbrook, James
Church, Benjamin
Conner, George
Cranston, William
Chucehook, David
Carson, Robert
Curtis, Henry
Champlin, Isaac
Corning, Benjamin
Corner, James
Cromell, Oliver
Cox, Joseph
Church, Israel
Cook, Ezekiel
Crowell, Seth
Clerk, John
Cooper, Mathew
Creech, Richard
Cook, Richard
Cooper, Nathaniel
Clerk, Isaac
Clerk, Tully
Clerk, Jonathan
Calhoun, Nathaniel
Crosby, Solomon
Clerk, Thomas
Congdon, Strautly
Clerk, Thomas
Cain, Thomas

Colman, Elisha
Coffin, Elisha
Cargal, William
Crosby, Daniel
Carea, Joseph
Carson, James
Caswell, John
Campbell, Philip
Crozier, William
Carew, Ezebiel
Champny, Benjamin
Chard, Ichabod
Clerk, Jacob
Cheevers, James
Collins, James
Combs, John
Cox, Samuel
Chillings, Thomas
Cheesebrook, Pierc
Congle, Muller
Clerk, John
Couch, James
Chevalier, Jean Gea
Clerk, William
Carpenter, Miles
Carpenter, John
Claypole, Samuel
Clayton, Edward
Crape, Abraham
Clerk, Alexander
Colson, Frederick
Clap, Twing Supply
Cranston, William
Cheesebrook, Andrew
Chase, Earle
Chase, Augustus
Calwell, Nicholas
Calder, James
Campbell, Alexander
Cotterall, David
Cunningham, Bartholo-
    mew
Chamberland, Charles
Chambers, Nancy
Cannady, James
Cox, Joseph
Cleaveland, David
Chamberlain, George
Carroll, John
Cook, Estric,

Cheavalin, John
Chapley, Joseph
Cape, Timothy
Cushing, Timnan
Cochran, Richard
Campbell, Jesse
Childs, Silas
Clerk, Thomas
Carowan, Piere
Cason, Samuel
Corsons, Batson
Carwell, John
Casian, Robert
Cook, John
Castel, John
Crown, George
Cook, Joseph
Cushing, Robert
Cushing, Joseph
Cocker, John
Casey, Richard
Campbell, Philip
Clerk, Lardner
Cobbs, Christopher
Cratterbrook, Joshua
Carson, William
Cochran, James
Crowzar, Nicholas
Colney, John
Champlin, Clerk
Colney, Abraham
Carbury Robert
Channell, Job
Coggeshall, John
Clerk, Pelig
Coxen, Thurmal
Came, Simon
Clements, Clement
Connell, John
Cornwell, William
Chapman, James
Clark, John
Cromwell, Oliver
Cowins, John
Canmer, Jacob
Calve, Parpi
Chivers, Bartholomew
Carter, William
Champlain, Francis
Cole, Benjamin

Cheesbrook, Andrew
Crandall, Henry
Conner, Robert
Crispin, William
Cheveland, Edward
Collins, James
Craft, Mathias
Cohlen, John
Campbell, James
Condon, Stafford
Collett, Thomas
Cavner, Anthony
Campbell, Alexander
Culver, Levi
Carlton, Thomas
Cowen, James
Crayton, James
Cheesman, Britton
Clemence, Michel
Cresean, John
Carey, John
Cobb, Nathaniel
Clapp, Supply
Combsbick, Nathaniel
Champion, Lines
Clerk, John
Charfill, William
Crosby, John
Curtis, Frederick
Condon, Patrick
Cavalier, James
Cadate, Louis Piere
Cassian, Gosper
Cokill, Gulliam
Cadate, Michael
Cox, John
Crosby, Daniel
Caswell, John
Coffin, Richard
Clarke, Joseph
Chapman, William
Carr, Isaac
Cullet, David
Clark, William
Carter, William
Cavman, Edward
Casher, Jacob
Cardends, Juanfernin
Cavello, Joseph Augustus
Covazeusa, Vizenteaugen

Carleton, Jean
Carles, Antonio
Coffin, Simon
Comick, Gilbert
Colley, Joseph
Connelly, John
Colley, Alexander
Cavman, John
Cong, Philip
Cotter, Anhgel
Combs, Mathew
Callaghan, Daniel
Comby, Joseph
Clove, John
Cawrse, John
Callagham, Barnaby
Crawford, John
Clarke, Jacob
Crawford, John
Coghill, Robert
Chase, Samuel
Cole, John
Clarke, Theodore
Cord, Andrew
Cancy, Richard
Clapp, Supply
Camaron, Edward
Christian, John
Coffee, William
Colburt, James
Cannon, Frances
Cavalier, Baptist
Cavalier, Thomas
Casper, Anthony
Cosgell, Christopher
Cobly, Timothy
Call, Charles
Coleman, Stephen
Clark, Church
Clark, Jubal
Chiller, Cadet
Coffin, Reuben
Clinasean, Jean
Chamberlain, Bird
Craft, Asesen
Clark, James
Collins, John
Cowdy, William
Challigue, Hurbin
Counice, Frances

Calon, Frances
Coulanseun, Pierre
Chenet, Lewis
Collec, Septoren
Cortland, Lewis
Cornean, Joseph
Church, Joseph
Crosley, William
Carlrsim, Justan
Craig, Thomas
Cobb, Jonathan
Canute, Jean
Cerbantin, John
Covet, Peter
Crorker, Bunsby
Craig, John
Clarke, Sylvester
Cox, Portsmouth
Colting, James
Chinks, David
Clarke, Noel
Cashwell, Jean
Cook, Benjamin
Cox, William
Chase, Ebenezer
Cooper, William
Call, Joseph
Coleman, James
Crocker, James
Cannon, John
Carney, Hugh
Castle, Thomas
Campbell, Robert
Carrington, Thomas
Cobb, Frances
Casan, Joseph
Crawford, Samuel
Crocker, Joshua
Crawley, Basil
Clarke William
Cook, Anthony
Clarke, Joseph
Cole, Thomas
Chapman, Lion
Casey, John
Cook, James
Clark, William
Cayaran, Oliver
Cousin, Joseph
Chien, Lasar

Chevalier, Julian
Codian, Lewis
Cotis, Noel
Cumnano, Joseam
Cooke, Samuel
Collins, Doan
Cooper, Nathanial
Cruse, Paul
Clarke, William
Crussell, Nicholas
Chaurine, Jovis
Cassey, Michael
Cash, Stephen
Casanovu, Joseph
Crough, Thomas
Coverly, John
Cousit, Lewis
Croix, Jean
Contout, Jean
Chalier, Perrie
Chasard Jean
Chese, Jean
Clayton, William
Chatfield, John
Chapman, Jeremiah
Curtis, Daniel
Curtis, Joseph
Cromwell, Richmond
Coburn, Eliphas
Carpenter, Willet
Corell, Eliphet
Cooper, Zabulan
Cuish, Philip
Cole, Walter
Castile, Joseph
Coffin, Zachariah
Columb, Julian
Case, Thomas
Cole, Joshua
Crim, John
Cornell, Mathew
Chapman, John
Chopman, Benjamin
Carvo, Frances
Carrllo, Jean
Cared, Petro
Cado, Jean
Cringea, Others
Cook, John
Cawer, Franch

Curry, Robert
Campbell, Thomas, 1
Campbell, Thomas, 2
Campbell, John
Clarke, Leonard
Cromwell, Robert
Cuningham, Isaac
Carr, John
Cole, Thomas
Carman, Benjamin
Cobb, John
Cobb, Thomas
Clarke, James
Cuffey, Benjamin
Crawford, Alias
Cross, Joseph
Clarke, Joshua
Creavy, Amos
Campbell, Frederick
Crow, Thomas
Chase, Alexander
Cole, Richard
Cuvbthson, James
Chapin, James
Chaplin, Lodowick
Cook, George
Cowbran, James
Cannon, Charles
Crawley, Cornelius
Caivins, Joseph
Carelton, Isaac
Coisten, David
Carey, John
Culvin, Samuel
Cochran, John
Canner, William
Chimney, Abel
Chencey, Benjamin
Cochran, John
Cornwell, Robert
Chester, William
Charbien, John
Cunningham, James
Couch, John
Couman, Nathaniel
Christan, William
Christin, William
Cresley, William
Cristin, George
Campbell, John

Chenaur, Christopher
Chalore, Pierri
Cornell, Jean
Courtny, Leonard
Corson, Pomeus
Crawford, Richard
Chester, Hiram
Carrall, Robert
Curry, Anthony
Carter, Levi
Coffin, Elias
Chipley, Leshere
Churchill, John
Caddington, John
Claring, Edward
Creepman, Thomas
Cunnican, James
Champlin, Jeffrey
Craypan, Benjamin
Clarke, Emanuel
Calfiere, Caplin
Chabbott, ——
Carr, Philip
Crapan, Christ
Chase, Loney
Cooke, Stephen
Chappell, John
Cahoone, John
Coustier, Jean
Cahoone, Jonathan
Cooper, William
Clarke Stephen
Cannady, William
Collingwood, Joseph
Codwith, John
Crowell, Sylvanus
Coffin, Edward
Carolin, Jean
Carolin, Joseph
Cubalod, Janeiese
Clarke, Timothy
Chapman, Samuel
Clarke, Nicholas
Cousnant, Frances
Coutt, John
Clark, Charles
Calbourn, Thomas
Code, Egnatus
Cobb, Christopher
Camp, Oscas

Clarke, Lewis
Clinton, David
Carson, Avil
Carson, Israel
Champion, Dore
Clinton, Samuel
Crossman, Joseph
Crow, Henry
Currell, Jacob
Chalkley, Samuel
Carmenell, William
Carmell, Benjamin
Cravetto, Albert
Carvell, John
Caird, Samuel
Coupra, Pierre
Curry, Augustus
Champray, Danforth
Cogeshall, William
Cobb, Christian
Corwell, Robert
Croft, Ebenezer
Chapman, Daniel
Cole, Abial
Cooper, Abraham
Carey, Joshua
Cook, Amos
Crow, Thomas
Coffin, Simon
Childs, James
Carrellton, William
Cummings, Benjamin
Chester, Hiram
Collough, Thomas
Conrad, George
Carr, John
Creassey, Amos
Coffin, Abel
Champery, Daniel
Currel, Jacob
Chapman, Daniel
Cambridge, Joseph
Coward, Zachariah
Cunningham, Cornelius
Carey, John
Church, Thomas
Case, John
Clarke, Job
Carson, William
Conwell, Robert

Craker, Gersham
Champion, Thomas
Challoner, John
Clanwell, Edward
Carroll, Perance
Conway, John
Carles, William
Crawford, Thomas
Curelus, Eden
Cunningham, William
Curry, William
Crow, Edward
Cavalier, George
Clever, Thomas
Carlisle, John
Cottrill, David
Crossman, John
Coleman, Nicholas
Crawford, Richard
Candie, Satarus
Crowell, William
Conner, John
Colver, Julian
Cobnan, Moses
Croudy, Christian
Cook, John
Collins, Abeader
Chapp, William
Curtis, William
Casp, John
Coventry, John
Cogan, Thomas
Clarke, Daniel
Clark, James
Colford, James
Caile, Thomas
Cook, James
Clarkson, Samuel
Codman, Christopher
Craft, Joseph
Canon, Samuel
Curtes, William
Chubb, Mathew
Corrigan, Bernard
Collings, John
Curwin, George
Cooper, Warren
Coffee, William
Casewell, Thomas
Collohan, Daniel

Clarke, Nicholas
Cawan, Pierre
Crocker, John
Carroway, Peter
Cann, John
Case, Seronte
Carey, Daniel
Costo, Antonio
Corrol, John
Cruth, Isaiah
Carson, Samuel
Cook, Frederick
Cable, Abel
Carson, Batison
Carson, Batterson
Callingham, James
Casey, Edward
Champion, Joseph
Carpenter, Richards
Craige, James
Cunningham, Joseph
Cook, John
Collier, Candal
Chubb, Mathew
Coarsin, John
Cox, Joseph
Codner, James
Chase, George
Carter, Thomas
Christian, Henry
Chittington, Benjamin
Cunningham, John
Coudon, Thomas
Casey, Richard
Connor, John
Corrigan, John
Conway, Thomas
Connolly, Patrick
Connolly, Samuel
Castle, Thomas
Carey, Richard
Contaney, Frederick
Culfey, William
Christian, John
Curtis, Frederick
Crookt, Hugh
Cherry, John
Crow, Mathew
Caveral, Thomas
Oraton, Thomas

Charoner, Jean
Cooping, Aaron
Craton, Thomas
Curtis, Frederick
Crosbury, Peter
Carland, Edward
Carmody, Edward
Colloy, Joseph
Coffin, Obediah
Clamron, Edward
Cullpper, Willis
Canes, Jacob
Cherry, William
Cornelius, Peter
Colinett, Lewis
Challoner, William
Colhoon, Miles
Cook, James
Clark, Thatcher
Crawford, John
Cape, Francis
Crane, Oliver
Celon, John
Cole, John
Crider, Michael
Crayton, Isaac
Cullen, William
Carson, Robert
Duforte, Jaque
Dunreas, Edane
Durant, Jaque
Deinay, Josper
Defangee, Francis
Dominica, Pierre
Davies, Ephraim
Donaldson, Daniel
Dobbs, Joseph
Duke, John
Duke, William
Diver, John
Day, Thomas
Darling, Richard
Dogget, Samuel
Deane, Josiah
Davies, Samuel
Doggett, Mathew
Days, Joseph
De Shille, Louis
Davids, Christopher
Dodd, William

Dwier, Timoth
Dickinson, John
Dowen, Hezekiah
Degoniere, Pierre
Daily, Samuel
Davies, William
Dwine, William
Doan, John
Dimon, James
Dennis, James
Dorgan, Patrick
Davies John
Demay, James
De Ggoslin, Revier
Dimson, Beebe
Dawson, Samuel
Dixon, Nicholas
Duffy, Thomas
Davis, Henry
Dempsep, Richard
Desiter, John
Davies, Edward
Dorson, Paul Paldon
Duran, Henry
Davies, Felton
Deakens, Jonathan
Dukerson, Isaac
Davies, William
Dwyer, John
Davis, Samuel
Deshea, Louis
Dennis, Benjamin
Dollaway, Nathaniel, 1
Dollaway, Nathaniel, 2
Denison, Beebe
Dennis, John
Daily, Samuel
Dwyman, William
Digon, Rene
Doin, Robert
Donaldson, W.
Duclos, Francis
Dennis, John
Dennison, Lemual
Dowen, Hezekiah
Dixon, John
Duchane, Michael
Davenport, Lott
Dean, Lewis
Darling, Henry

Dowdey, James	Dennis, Deverick	Dade, Isaac
Dyer, Roger	Davis, John	Doyle, Peter
Demmay, Sosish	Dyer, James	Dublands, James
De Wolf, Stephen	Dillons, Joseph	Dudley, Abner
Donan, Solomon	Delano, Zebulon	Dogget, Samuel
Dyer, Fitch	Downs, Prince	Diber, David
Demeny, David	Day, Thomas	Deane, George
Dann, Samuel	Degree, William	Duncan, George
Deming, Israel	Debong, Michael	Day, Thomas
Dexter, Benjamin	Degree, Piere Guisigope	Damon, Reuben
Davies, John	Daniel, John	Dawn, Thomas
Darling, Henry	Delaboney, Demand	Dickerson, Edward
Dyer, Samuel	Dunlot, Allen	Dennis, Joseph
Duplesey, Francis	Duff, John	Davies, Benjamin
Dunn, Joseph	Drewry, Thomas	Donalds, Anthony
Dillingham, Edward	Dailey, Patrick	Dixon, Daniel
Davies, Richard	Duran, Charles	Dogget Samuel
Dwyer, Timothy	Delone, Henry	Diers, Joseph
Ducloy, Martin	Duke, Chemuel	Dogget, Mathew
Dyer, Alexander	Donalin, Nicholas	Drawere, Samuel
Dohn, Josiah	Denike, Daniel	Duncan, John
Dyer, Jonathan	Doudney, Jay	Dwyer, Timothy
Dyer, Hat	Davies, John	Donken, George
Dixon, William	Davies, William	Dailey, James
Dennis, William	Dean, Orlando	Deal, Isaac
Diah, Jona	Douval, Thomas	Downeneroux, Frances
Davis, Christopher	Doyle, Peter	Downs, Nathaniel
Davies, Henry	Dunkwater, Piere	Dehart, Jacob
Dunwell, Stephen	Durphey, Patrick	Daily, James
Duclos, Francis	Dubtoe, Henry	Dallahide, James
Dyer, Hubert	Davies, John	Dole, John
Davies, Christopher	Dimon, John	Doleby, Elisha
Dean, Orlando	Doyle, William	Dickinson, Ichabod
Dimon, Benjamin	Daily, James	Dongan, John
Dixon, William	Douglass, Robert	Dussle, William
Dawne, John	Daniel, Christopher	Domreau, Jean
Day, John	Davidson, John	De Course, Jean
Davies, Thomas	Devericks, John	Dedd, Francois
Day, William	Davies, Samuel	Dorgan, Patrick
Duval, Jacob	Dolbuy, Elisha	Darling, William
Docherty, Hugh	Dorcey, Nathaniel	Drowne, Simeon
Docherty, Henry]	Denroron, David	Dickinson, Edward
Duverick, James	Deverick, James	Day, Joseph
Duncon, James	Delevan, Amos	Davies, John
Davies, Benjamin	Dailey, Benjamin	Dennis, Joseph
Dexter, Benjamin	Davies, Richard	Downs, Prince
Dexter, Simon	Duskin, Anthony	Duval, Pardon
Dorgan, Patrick	Dade, Isaac	Deboy, Peter
Dodd, William	Duscanson, Robert	Damison, Benjamin
Deamond, Benjamin	Doggle, Timothy	Duckie, Jean

Duran, Lewis
Delace, Domingo
Delevas, Pierre
Dadica, Jean
Degune, Lewis'
Davis, William
Dean, Levi
Dexter, Aaron
Dixon, Christopher
Dunning, Mathew
Dowling, Henry
Derry, William
Deawer, John
Dearing, Daniel
Davis, John
Davis, Thomas
Drew, Abadiah
Duless, Michael
Day, Michael
Dixon, Robert
Dissell, Michael
Davies, Eliga
Douting, Iseno
Downey, John
Doherty, John
Dunn, Peter
Dutchett, Rowl
Domran, Edward
Doherty, Thomas
Denham, Robert
Donming, John
Dunn, Arthur
Delany, Edward
Darrough, Charles
Davies, John
Dodge, James
Daniss, Samuel
Dunnope, Thomas
Dailey, Robert
Daniel, John
Downing, Peter
Dannivan, William
Douglass, William
Deale, Elias
Dillow, John
Duflield, Thomas
Dubison, Jean
Delgada, Frances
Daily, William
Dixon, Nicholas

Deane, Thomas
Donham, Benjamin
Dixon, Robert
Drawberry, James
Dixon, Christian
Deale, Elias
Davidson, Samuel
Diabeary, Elerouand
Darcey, W.
Doherty, John
Dunlope, John
Dunslope, Allen
Drayton, James
Dunlope, Thomas
Deal, John
Duffey, Ezekiel
Dunison, John
Daniel, John
Davies, John
Davies, Elijah
Dixon, James
Dixon, James
Davis, James
Dupee, Ehenne
Depue, Lewis
Duffey, Doulram
Dunkin, James
Darby, Benjamin
Douglas, Frances
Delare, Gare
De Frankfort, Gilliem
Davis, Curtis
Downing, John
Dorgan, Timothy
Dennis, Paine
Dens, John
Dennis, Moses
Du Puo, Jean
Dehango, Pratus
Dagget, Silas
Dower, John
Devaratte, Jeane
Doxburg, James
Dunlopp, Archibald
Doisu, Frances
Dabnican, Gulam
Deschem, Pierre
Degle, Jean
Disaablan, Piere
Dingle, Robert

Dupue, France
Davie, Pierre
Durvana, Jonathan J.
Dart, Robert
Dimon, Charles
Dougue, Peter C.
Drake, Thomas
Drabb, Murray
Devay, Gabriel
Devoy, Thomas
Darby, William
Dowden, William
Dumravan, Terrence
Daccarmell, John
Devise, Francis
Dagure, John
Dora McDora, John
Dora, Frances
De Hester, Thomas
Dawson, Samuel
Devay, Isaac
Denauf, Avery
Divie, Victori
Davan, Bastian
Dayton, William
Dyer, Nathan
Doseemer, Joseph
Dupee, Michael
Dean, Benjamin
Darley, Thomas
Dean, Philip
Daveick, James
Davies, John
Dunton, William
Durham, Sylvester
Derry, Daniel
Duncon, William
Daniel, Lewis
Doget, George
Dredge, William
Danby, Thomas
Dingo, Elisha
Dickerson, Thomas
Dewereux, Robert
Dennister, Jean
Dickinson, Benjamin
Deverux, James
Devoe, Daniel
Desseno, Jacob
Donald, Barton

24

Demen, Element
Deville, Joseph
Davies, Samuel
Dewof, Simon
Donies, Deverough
Duphane, Thomas
Dluice, Etemin
Davis, Charles
Davis, Lewis
Dubois, John
Davies, Lewis
Dill, Thomas
Drown, William
Davis, Benjamin
Dealing, Daniel
Delcostar, Joseph
Davis, Isaac
Dennis, Jonas
Delore, Anthony
Delas, Anthony
Davies, Jesey
Dung, Thomas
Dowray, John
Dolbier, John
Dalley, Jeremiah
Dunmerhay, John
Dnnnam, Sylvester
Dick, Archibald
Ducker, Archibald
Dyer, Robert
Duvae, Jacob
Dunning, John
Dunning, William
Da Las, Anthony
Dugree, Franes
Draullard, Jean
Donguen, Anthony
Derboise, Jean
Dunhire, John
Davis, Nathan
Deane, Archibald
Dobiee, John
Davis, Benjamin
Dority, Joseph
Decostor, Joseph
Delary, Gaspan
Driver, John
Davies, Thomas
Davies, John
Demelot, Jean

Drew, John
Deck, Benorey
Durphy, Israel
Dickenson, Benjamin
Dunbar, James
Dyer, Patrick
Denoe, John
Durand, Glased
Duss, Andrew
Deralia, Manuel
Duflin, Michael
Dennis, John
Devey, Honor
Debland, James
Derorow, Daniel
Deans, John
Eldridge, Daniel
Eldridge, Thomas
Elderkin, Luther
Edmondo, Downes
Elderton, Daniel
Eticore, Anthony
Eton, Joseph
Eveane, Francis
Eugalind, Joseph
Eugalind, Francis
Ewell, William
Ewell, Thomas
Ewing, James
Edwards, Charles
Elridge, Nathaniel
Ewing, Thomas
Ede, William
Edgar, John
Esk, James
Edwards, Michael
Edwards, William
Edmund, John
Ekelston, James
Elns, Stephen
Edmund, Henry
Earle, Isaac
Elliot, Joseph
Elias, Benjamin
Elderkin, Jean
Eronte, Martin
Elias, Jonathan
Elwell, Samuel
Elkins, James
Earle, Pardon

Eskridge, Walford
Eli, John
Ebben, Joseph
Each, David
Everson, George
Edwards, Edward
Easterbrook, Charles
Edwards, Alexander
Eddison, Thomas
Eaves, John
Earle, Benjamin
Elridge, Ever
Edwards, John
Engrum, John
Euston, Ned
Eldridge, James
Ebinstone, John
Edgar, Jessee
Emery, George
Elder, Nathan
Eachforsh Samuel
Eves, Benjamin
Elliott, Nathaniel
Emilgon, Jean
Evins, John
Elith, Benjamin
Evens, William
Elwell, John
Ewing, Thomas
Eyes, Christian
Evena, Pierre
Evena, Peni
Earle, Richard
Edwards, Michael
Everson, John
Edgarton, James
Echeverial, Manuel de
Ergnia, Ignaus
Eebeveste, Avico
Echave, Amorois
Echanegud, Frances
Echeranid, Lorendo
Echangucia, Joseph
Echenarria, Feruim
Expassa, Juan Vizente
Echoa, Joseph Nicolas
Echeserria, Frances
Echeserria, Ignacia
Eldred, Aldub
Edwards, Rolla

Ellsworth, Theodore
Edwards, Thomas
Edwards, William
Eleves, William
Elliott, Cornelius
Edwards, James
Everly, Robert
Eggleston, Samuel
Etherton, Thomas
Edbron, ———
Evins, David
Elliot, Daniel
Edgar, William
Emanuel, James
Even, Lewis
Edgar, Thomas
Elbridge, Jonathan
Edwards, Daniel
Erexson, John
Epworth, Samuel
Eggleston, James
Edwards, Henry
Earle, Lewis
Elgin, Richard
Ellwell, Samuel
Ellwell, Isaac
Earle, Pardon
Everall, Ebenezer
Elliot, John
Easterbrook, Amos
Eason, Michael
Ellwell, Samuel
Eoon, John
Evens, Even
Eyres, Francis
Esward, Anthony
Edgar, William
Emanuel, James
Ecley, Thomas
Edelin, Butter
Eldridge, Ezra
Ewen, Peter
Ellery, Nicholas
Eugannin, Francis
Eldridge, Daniel
Ellis, Jonathan
Evans, Pierc
Ellison, John
Ellison, John
Eadoe, David

Evans, Elias
Eldridge, William
Eadoe, David
Everett, Jeremiah
Edgerton, Philip
Egrant, James
Falker, George
Finney, Jonathan
Fling, John
Fuller, Thadeus
Follows, Stephen
Fuganey, Joseph
Fellows, James
Fillear, Jean Francis
Finagan, Bartholomew
Fury, John
Fore, Daniel
Fitch, Josiah
Fernando, Joseph
Ferartd, Joseph
Ferbon, Domigo
Finch, David
Fisher, William
Follows, Stephen
Fowler, James
Falam, Henry
Fennell, Thomas
Friend, Post
Friers, James
Fortune, James
Fancien, Jean
Fravi, John
Fulton, Thomas
Fuller, Joseph
Fist, Solomon
Fish, John
Fouvnary, Pruden
Fisk, John
Fall, Robert
Folsom, John
Felter, David
Forsyth, Timothy
Fowler, Gideon
Fennell, Caleb
Freeman, Thomas
Freeman, David
Foster, Boston
Folston, John
Fenwell, Cable
Finner, Jeremiah

Fallen, Thomas
Foster, John
Fomster, Joseph
Fletcher, John
Fisham, John
Figg, Nathaniel
Francis, Thomas
Freing, Thomas
Francis, John
Ford, Bartholomew
Francis, John
Fluort, Michael
Fravers, John F.
Fry, James
Finer, George
Fowler, James
Falls, Henry
Frasier, Joseph
Francois, Jean
Foy, William
Fairfield, Benjamin
Futter, Iman
Faber, John
Ferre, Joseph
Fermang, Piere
Furer, Ubain
Frebal, Iman
Fabalue, Jean Paul
Fougne, Lewis
Fairfield, John
Fettian, Elisha
Finney, Jonathan
Foster, Josiah
Fiarde, Frederick
Fowler, Michael
Ferrea, Joseph
Franco, Juan
Fish, Nathaniel
Folland, Francis
Fish, Asel
Fisk, John
Foot, Samuel
Fennell, Cable
Fuller, James
Foster, John
Fuller, Thomas
Fauntroy, Robert
Francisco, Manuel
Fonster, Edward
Fisher, Robert

26

Fielding, W.
Fergoe, Mathew
Fielding, William
Frazier, Andrew
Fowler, John
Fisher, Isaac
Fox, Ebenezer
Fowler, Joseph
Fogg, Thomas
Follett, Jonathan
Fist, John
Frasier, Thomas
Fostman, Ephraim
Fernon, Ephraim
Fry, Robert
Feebe, Joseph
Finney, Jonathan
Foster, Edward
Foster, Josiah
Fife, John
Fisk, John
Finney, Seth
Fielding, William
Faulke, Jacob
Frasier, Thomas
Fere, David
Fisher, Jonathan
Fish, Nathaniel
Frost, John
Fisher, William
Fisher, Nathaniel
Foster, Jebediah
Fairfield, John
Fry, Robert
Fosdic, Thomas
Fish, Daniel
Foster, Josiah
Frask, Nathaniel
Ferney, Mathew
Frienda, Shadrick
Finesy, Dennis
Ferret, Lewis
Fisher, Robert
Frailey, Jacob
Frazer, Andrew
Fitch, Theopolus
Faithful, William
Forker, George
Foster, Conrad
Foster, Andrew

Freeman, Thomas
Foster, Jacob
Fling, Edward
Foster, John
Ficket, John
Frett, Josea
Frick, Anthony
Fellows, Nathaniel
Fisher, Simon
Filler, Patrick
Fray, William
Faroe, John
Finn, Dennis
Freeman, John
Fowler, John
Freeman, David
Fary, Thomas
Foy, John Butler
Franklin, Pernell
Footman, John
Ford, Daniel
Felt, Benjamin
Frailey, Jacob
Field, Charles
Fordham, George
Fernal, Noah
Files, Benjamin
Freway, Julian
Ford, Bartholomew
Fincher, John
Feller, Martin
Frith, Josiah
Foot, Zakiel
Fimsey, John
Fisher, Robert
Fithin, William
Fling, William
Furse, John
French, Michael
Freebal, William
Francis, Thomas
Foster, Heury
Flinn, John
Fisher, Archibald
Freeman, Humphrey
Ford, George
Frost, Joseph
Fox, William, 1
Foster, John
Fox, William, 2

Foster, Henry
Frost, Joseph
Floyd, Berry
Foyer, Jared
Fitchett, Henry
Ford, George
Foster, Asa
Foster, Ephraim
Fortaud, Emanuel
Fevmandez, Manuel
Ferote, Ehemre
Fullum, George
Ford, John
Fretto, John
Ford, Philip
Ford, Bartholomew
Frances, John
Fordham, Benjamin
Fatem, Henry
Forster, Frances
Farmer, William
Fenton, John
Ferris, Paul
Ferris, Conway
Furguson, Abner
Forgue, Vancom
Fester, William
Forgough, Mathew
Fusilen, Charles
Fish, Ezekiel
Fitts, Christopher
Frisby, Ebenezer
Freeman, Henry
Farland, John
Furguson, Abraham
Foster, Nathaniel
Filton, Ward
Foster, John
Eord, John
Fox, William
Ferril, Kenedy
Fairfield, Ashan
Foulyer, James
Fulton, James
Freeman, Zebedial
Fernanda, Frances
Finney, Thomas
Fuller, Thomas
Franks, Christopher
Finley, Frances

Frances, Scobud
Foot, Daniel
Frances, Thomas
Felpig, Peter
Felpig, John
Fitzgerald, Patrick
Foster, John
Fouber, John
Freeman, Henry
Ford, Philip
Falkender, Ephraim
Foresyth, Hugh
Firmie, Robert
Foster, Nicholas
Finley, James
Frankie, Anthony
Ford, William
Finn, John
Field, John
Firth, Joseph
Foster, William
Frume, Peter
Fulger, Joshua
Fulger, Reuben
Foubert, Frances
Fubre, Joseph
Frances, Joseph
Foster, George
Fernray, Fountain
Frasier, John
Forrest Nathaniel
Fitz, Patrick Faroh
Fulger, Stephen
Fifer, Edwin
Furguson, Samuel
Fort, John
Fitzgerald, Edward
Forquer, Samuel
Francis, William
Fanch, Frances
Frances, Fortain
Ferton, Pierre
Farrean, Michael
Freasi, Pierre
Fitch, Ebenezer
Fleet, Thomas
Fitch, Peter
Fitch, Timothy
Fitch, Jedediah
Frisby, Isaac

Fuller, Benjamin
French, Jonathan
Freeman, Charles
French, James
Ford, Martin
Fryske, Abijah
Forbes, Peter
Fortasa, Anthony
Fernandis, Thomas
Frankes, Michael
Fisher, Abraham
Francis, Thomas
Farrow, William
Gross, Michael
Gamble, Joseph
Gilchrist, Robert
Gill, Philip
Grame, Robert
Gale, Jonas
Gorhan, James
Garret, Antonio
Green, John
Gratton, William
Garnett, John
Gamble, James
Gibbs, Charles
Gibbins, John
Gay, Solomon
Grogan, John
Gardner, Alexander
Gawner, Thomas
Govier, Joseph
Grilley, Thomas
Gates, Charles
Gross, Tonoss
Godfrey, William
Gorham, Jonathan
Gold, Ebenezer
Green, Joseph
Gordon, James
Green, John
Gandy, William
Gibbons, John
Guorde, Elisha
Gorham, Shubert
Griffin, Elias
Glinn, Thomas
Green, Greenbury
Giles, Samuel
Gotea, Jean

Garrett, William
Goddard, Thomas
Gear, John
Grant, Thomas
Gothe, George
Grandall, Adam
Gillespie, William
Gasker, Jacob
Guiness, Joseph
Garret, Michael
Green, William
Gandee, William
Grotfield, Peleg
Gardner, Thomas
Gardner, Dominic
Godfrey, Joseph
Green, Rufus
Geddes, Robert
Gardner, Joseph
Grierson, William
Gisburn, William
Gibb, George
Green, Elisha
Gault, John
Gandle, William
Gardner, William
Garish, Paul
Garish, James
Gasett, Daniel
Goodnow, Eli
Gray, William
Grose, Jonah
Gowell, George
Gray, Simon
Godfry, Francis
Gold, John
Garland, John
Gwinnup, William
Gowell, George
Graham, Samuel
Glenn, Gabriel
Gamband, James
Gillot, David
Grey, Samuel
Gardner, Uriah
Gilson, Nathaniel
Grover, Thomas
Gunnup, William
Gill, John
Giles, William

28

Glates, Charles
Griskin, Philip
Griffin, Daniel
Greenway, Joseph
Gibson, James
Greencafe, Enoch
Gascin, Job
Gallager, Andrew
Gandway, Francis
Grace, Mathew
Grinn, Peter
Guinep, William
Goodwin, Gideon
Godfrey, William
Garland, John
Gardiner, William
Godfrey, Simon
Goodman, Francis
Gamble, James
Gardner, William
Goodrich, Jesse
Green, Allen
Goodrich, Elizer
Gross, Simon P.
Gregory, Stephen
Grottis, Andrew
Ginnies, Peter
Going, John
Greeman, Isaac
Greenoth, John
Gray, Samuel
Gardner, Joseph
Garret, Isaac
Greenwell, Malum
Gardner, Silas
Gilladen, John
Godfrey, William
Goyear, Jean
Gardon, Domonico
Glerner, Thomas
Gillerd, John
Godfrey, Samuel
Gardner, William
Gooding, Lemuel
Green, Henry
Goodley, George
Gardner, James
Goodby, George
Griffin, Peter
Grinn, Peter

Goodwin, Gideon
Griere, Isaac
Gardner, William
Gardner, Alexander
Gambo, Peter
Gray, Dingley
Georgean, George
Griffin, Moses
Green, John
Gilleny, Richard
Guilley, John
Gifford, Archibald
Green, John
Grant, Alexander
Gulirant, William
Garrett, Jaques
Griere, Mather
Guin, Peter
Guinet, Joseph
Cowell, George
Gilchrist, George
Goove, Abel
Gordon, James
Green, John
Grenach, Ebenezer
Griggs, John
Gordon, Andrew
Gibbertson, Edward
Greeness, John
Grant, William
Godfrey, William
Gallard, John
Gray, Simeon
Gallaspie, John
Goreham, Jonathan
Griflin, Alexander
Greenfield, Richard
Griflin, James
Griggs, James
Garico, Manolet
Griswold, Elijah
Green, William
Gonire, Lewis
Gordan, Andrew
Gaylor, John
Greene, James
Goodwick, James
Goodrich, Solomon
Gandy, John
Gordon, Peter

Gabrill, Francis
Grassing, Thomas
Grout, Michael
Gassers, John
Graham, Alexander
George, Isaac
Glesson, William
Garrett, John
Grigg, James
Gray, Alexander
Grier, Charles
Grosper, Peter
Glosses, Michael
Griflin, James
Goff, Patrick
Griffith, William
Gardner, William
Granb, Ebenezer
Gray, Dingley
Garriway, Thomas
Gissia, Francis
Gilmont, John
Giflis, William
Gregory, David
Goram, Jonathan
Grothou, John
Gill, John
Gardner, James
Green, Robert
Goose, Abel
Godfrey, William
Gregory, Stephen
Goram, Jonathan
Gay, William
Griffin, Joseph
Gurdell, Anthony
Gearde, ——
Gibbs, Charles
Green, Joseph
Greene, James
Gage, Mathew
Gelstone, Hugh
Greene, John
Garrit, Joseph
Golston, William
Glaied, Jean
Gardela, Antony
Gilmore, John
Greene, John
Gibbs, Charles

29

Godfrey, Thomas
Gardiner, Silas
Green, John
Garrison, Jacob
Gibson, George
Green, Elijah
Gloud, Daniel
Glover, Jonathan
Gugg, Nathanial
Garsea, Roman
Gullion, Joseph
Glease, Jean
Green, John
Gardner, Thomas
Goodwin, George
Gardner, Samuel
Goodfrey, Simon
Green, William
Gomer, Robert
Greenleaf, Abner
Gascin, Job
Gegleston, James
Guster, George
Gloss, Edward
Gibson, Andrew
Gleassea, John
Gardner, Alexander
Gordon, Stephen
Gallway, William
Graham, Robert
Gusbero, Franes
Griffith, James
Greenway, Parten
Girca, Joseph
Gage, Isaac
Gage, Stephen
Gibson, Benjamin
Guivure, Jonathan B.
Gross, Benjamin
Greenwold, Robert
Guneuse, Jean
Girand, Baptist
Grenyard, Ebenezer
Grudge, Samuel
Goute, Augustus
Grubt, John
Gillmay, Toby
Gage, Herman
Giles, Thomas
Gray, Joseph

Greenville, William
Gillen, Jean B.
Guilber, Pierre
Greene, James
Gardner, Larry
Goquie, ——
Gootman, James
Gill, William
Guenar, Bense
Gillis, John
Garrett, Richard
Gotson, Charles
Geffrey, Clare
Gibbons, John
Gimrey, Thomas
Gloaque, James
Garley, Joseph
Godt, Pierre
Giron, Jean
Garrier, Louis C.
Gult, Souran
Goertin, Vincent
Ganart, Pierre
Gray, Joseph
Guason, John
Gason, Simon
Gunder, Julian
Gavney, Peter
Goat, Thomas
Gaurmon, Samuel
Gardner, Robert
Grouan, Joseph
Goutiere, Francis
Gaur, Paul
George, George
Garty, William
Granby, William
Garey, John
Goodwin, Ozeas
Gallys, Anthony
Gararads, Hosea
Guea, John
Garo, Jean
Garrow, John
Goson, Christian
Goss, William
Giles, Samuel
Giles, John
Gore, Jesse
Godfrey, William

Godfrey, Nathaniel
Godfrey, Thomas
Grennis, William
Garrison, Jacob
Glover, William
Guillen, Edwin
Garner, Silas
Garner, ——
Garlena, Barney
Guan, Syras
Ginnow, Jean
Goodall, Pierre
Gurad, Pierre
Gilbert, Timothy
Green, John
Gibbs, John
Gord, John
Gunteer, Jean
Green, John
Grafton, William
Gillison, John
Gibbs, John
Gowyall, Henry
Graimes, David
Guay, John
Gray, Franes
Geweas, Jean
Gormia, Joseph
Gasse, Manot
Gabriel, Franes
Gabria, Endria
Galina, Joseph
Govell, Sylvester
Goddard, Ebenezer
Goddard, Nicholas
Gayford, Charles
Greene, Samuel
Grissell, Edward
Gibbons, Charles
Griswold, John
Griffin, Jasper
Green, Elijah
Gillispie, David
Gason, Simon
Garnett, Silvester
George, George
Granada, L. A.
Gater, Frances
Glorman, William
Gundas, Antonio

Giddron, Stephen
Grogon, Joseph
Griffin, Moses
Griffen, Moses
Griffin, Rosetta
Garrison, Joseph
Greenwood, Jacob
Gilbert, George
Goodfry, Eli
Garretson, John
Goodwin, Daniel
Galley, Richard
Grymes, George
Gathand, Jean Joseph
Grover, Thomas
Goudin, Francis
Gray, James
Guvare, Francis
Goodwin, Charles
Grove, Stephen
Gerrard, Hooper
Henry, Robert
Holland, John
Hollen, Nicholas
Hooper, Ezekiel
Huston, James
Howard, Thomas
Heft, George
Harris, Charles
Humphries, Clement
Howard, William
Hankley, Peter
Hazard, John
Hisburn, John
Hunn, Mathew
Hint, Jonathan
Hautley, Samuel
Hubbard, James
Hunn, Ephraim
Hawser, Jacob
Huddle, William
Higgins, Stoutly
Heysham, William
Howbern, James
Hanagan, Stephen
Hujuon, Pierre
Hallet, James
Home, James
Hellman, Mathias
Hand, Joseph

Hammond, Jacob
Hines, James
Hilliard, Joseph
Handy, Thomas
Hook, John
Hawkins, Jabez
Himsly, Benjamin
Haddock, Benjamin
Henley, Leemand
Hewett, Jesse
Hewett, Abial
Hibbett, Diah
Horne, Samuel
Hughes, Peter
Hallet, Benjamin
Hudson, John
Herrick, Ephraim
Hampested, Daniel
Hardy, Joseph
Hammond, David
Huffman, Conrad
Harkins, Thomas
Hutchinson, Thomas
Hertros, Augustin
Hammond, Allen John
Harris, John
Hawkins, Thomas
Hathaway, Russell
Hathaway, Jacob
Hedges, Heraclus
Hathaway, Woolsey
Hathaway, Burton
Hoogland, Nicholas
Hartus, Thomas
Handy, Thomas
Hall, Thomas
Hatch, William
Hunt, Eiphas
Hall, Willis
Hoppins, Lowe
Halley, Joseph
Henderson, William
Hill, John
Hales, Mathew
Hodges, Hercules
Huntington, Elisha
Hawkins, Thomas
Holloway, Michael
Harkey, Solomon
Hooper, John

Halley, Samuel
Hassett, John
Hawstick, Jacob
Hawkins, James
Howard, Absolam
Hoskins, Jehu
Humphrey, Richard
Henyard, Dennis
Helbow, Edmund
Henderson, Alexander
Horn, Joseph
Hubbard, Dolphin
Hooper, John
Halbort, David
Haldron, William
Hall, Ebenezer
Hate, William
Harte, Jacob De
Hallett, Benjamin
Hartley, Samuel
Hallibert, Thomas
Ham, Jonathan
Hawkins, Christopher
Hanagan, James
Herson, Robert
Hughes, Greenford
Hewengs, John
Hodgson, Samuel
Hengry, Robert
Hopkins, Michael
Hopkins, Caleb
Hall, Richard
Hayes, John
Harris, John
Horne, Jacob
Hallett, James
Hooper, John
Hopper, John
Hodges, Hercules
Hathaway, Jacob
Howe, Thomas
Hutilet, Jean
Harlin, Charles
Huss, Charles
Hardy, James
Hawkins, Jabez
Hook, John
Hoppins, Levi
Hartman, Jacob
Hoffman, Conrad

Hall, Aaron
Harmon, John
Hicpey, Daniel
Hanes, Patrick
Hunter, George
Hanegan, John
Huss, Isaac
Hodge, Hugh
Hopkins, William
Hinman, William
Hinch, Peter
Halman, Henry
Hokey, Lemuel
Hensey, Patrick
Hanes, Samuel
Hamond, Benjamin
Harris, James
Hanson, Henry
Hendray, Archibald
Heart, Gilbert
Hooper, Michael
Harris, Robert
Harket, John
Hill, Thomas
Hanes, Josiah
Higgins, George
Harmitage, Shulbert
Harris, Hugh
Harris, Robert
Harfun, John
Hosea, Jean
Hanfield, Gideon
Hopping, Richard
Hires, Christian
Harbley, Daniel
Huggins, John
Hammond, Benjamin
Hooper, Michael
Hunt, Jessee
Hagan, Caraway
Hatbor, Charles
Hand, Joseph
Hill, Thomas
Huffman, Conner
Haynes, Peter
Hunter, Turtle
Halley, John
Hunt, Robert
Hazard, Benjamir
Haggarty, James

Hunt, John
Hall, Samuel
Hardy, George
Hall, Aaron
Hatch, Nailer
Harris, Charles
Hargus, Abraham
Hyde, Abraham Smith
Hayden, Benjamin
Hawston, John
Harrison, Gilbert
Hose, Henry
Hall, Thomas
Horne, Ralf
Hall, John
Howe, John
Hogsart, Alexander
Hobbs, Henry
Hick, Michael
Harden, Turner
Hopkins, John
Hodge, Ebenezer
Hobby, Jacob
Hobby, Nathaniel
Higgins, Ichabod
Hamilton, John
Hart, Cornelius
Hertson, Robert
Humphries, John
Hopkins, Stephen
Hardy, Thomas
Hallanghan, James
Hays, William
Harris, Joseph
Henry, Michael
Holmes, Nathaniel
Howard, Ebenezer
Higgins, William
Horne, John
Hoogland, Nicholas
Hammond, John
Hudson, Fawions
Hammoad, David
Honlap, Warren
Hosey, John
Hudson, Phineas
Higgins, William
Hinnran, Nathaniel
House, George
Harley, Solomon

Hoane, Edwin
Hammond, William
Holmes, Nathaniel
Hardy, Joseph
Holt, Samuel
Hamilton, William
Harborough, Augustus
Hunter, Alexander
Harkazy, Thomas
Holloway, Wyburn
Homer, Jacob
Hillory, Nicholas
Hatt, Andrew
Hatch, Jason
Hallwell, Charles
Hottahon, James
Handy, Thomas
Hatch, Prince
Harley, Selden
Hoffman, Cornelius
Haynes, Peter
Hallahan, James
Horoe, Michael
Hussey, Joseph
Huet, John
Hawke, William
Halts, Jesse
Howell, Luke
Hawkins, John
Hitchband, Joseph
Harens, Thomas
Harman, John
Heskils, Stephen
Hughes, Thomas
Hughes, Greenbury
Hilton, Nathaniel
Hicks, Baptist
Hage, Anthoy Dela
Herart, Sanson
Harding, Nathaniel
Hood, Daniel
Hurand, Joseph
Hardin, Lewis
Hammond, Homer
Hughes, John
Herewux, Philip
Hattway, Sherdrac
Henderson, Ephraim
Huson, Nathaniel
Huson, Israel

Hubbard, William
Haybud, George
Hudman, John
Hill, Joshua
Holmes, Isaac
Hays, Patrick
Hays, David
Hamilton, Henry
Howell, Michael
Homer, William
Harris, John
Hiron, Samuel
Herring, Michael
Hall, Isaac
Hamilton, William
Huson, Negro
Hanks, Every
Hammond, Joseph
Hetherington, John
Hale, William
Hiskman, Samuel
Hayes, Thomas,
Hearth, Joseph
Holmes, Thomas
Holmes, Thomas
Hitch, Loren
Hasker, John
Hamber, William
Howland, William
Hyde, Jedediah
Harman, Richard
Holly, Grandless
Harwood, John
Ham, Levi
Hockless, Joseph
Hughes, Abraham
Hood, Daniel
Hammond, Elijah
Hayes, John
Howell, James
Hilton, Hale
Halley, Ephraim
Halley, Joseph
Hovey, Joseph
Hurd, Joseph
Hurd, Benjamin
Higgins, Samuel
Hurlbut, Asca
Herrick, John
Hackett, John

Hall, Millen
Henry, John
Howland, Daniel
Harlow, Biron
Hall, James
Hurd, Simon
Hirich, John
Huggins, John
Hemingway, Jerid
Howell, Walter
Harris, Edward
Hose, Henry
Hall, Thomas
Horne, Ralf
Hall, John
How, John
Hogshart, Alexander
Howard, John
Humphries, William W
Hannings, John
Harris, George
Holden, William
Halsey, William
Hall, Joseph
Holt, Charles
Howell, Thomas
Harvey, John
Holliday, William
Higgins, William
Hubbard, Joel
Hubbard, Moses
Holdridge, Thomas
Hitchcock, Edward
Hall, London
Hough, Ebenezer
Hatchway, Edward
Honeyman, William
Hemana, Odera
Henumway, Enos
Harris, Francis
Husband, George
Hives, Arthur
Hitcher, Robert
Hoggan, Stephen
Heart, Samuel
Hawker, Jacob
Harris, Nathaniel
Hook, George
Herrow, Robert
Henry, John

Hawker, John
Hunt, Joseph
Hislop, John
Higgano, Isaac
Hawker, Samuel
Hamilton, John
Haruage, John
Hawkins, Andrew
Hamilton, John
Highlenede, John
Harbert, Neil
Holmes, James
Heath, Sesen
Higlander, Henry
Hartshorn, James
Hinch, Peter
Harrett, Lewis
Harron, William
Haney, John
Hammond, Elijah
Hanwood, Jonathan
Halwell, Benjamin
Hassa, Jacob
Hamilton, Empson
Horsme, Charles
Hambell, Reuben
Howell, Ebenezer
Hand, Elias
Hand, Gidron
Holmsted, George
Hussty, Jacob
Harrison, Elijah
Hand, Elijah
Husband, John
Hunter, Robert
Haselton, Peter
Harbine, John
Henry, William
Hargeshonor, Joel
Harrison, John
Hargons, Jacob
Haynes, William
Hatchway, Edward
Hashley, Michael
Hogworth, Jacob
Hoyde, Benjamin
Howell, Jesse
Hinman, Aaron
Herrick, John
Hebell, Jack

Harvey, Elisha
Harris, Robert
Hughes, Joseph
Hanwright, John
Howard, William
Holland, William
Hammond, James
Henry, John
Haglus, John
Howell, John
Hibell, John
Heageork, Samuel
Handy, Livi
Henderson, Joseph
Hoag, Willirk
Hail, Ebenezer
Hutchinson, John
Howard, Richard
Henry, James
Hayman, Nicholas
Harris, James
Hovard, Noah
Hancock, Abraham
Haynes, Thomas
Haynes, Joseph
Hyer, Vincent
Hutchens, Zachariah
Holland, William
Hatch, Edward
Howell, William
Harrison, Charles
Holland, Michael
Herbert, Thomas
Harris, John
Hogan, Roger
Harrington, Daniel
Hogan, Stephen
Paupe, Michael
Hard, Jean
Hitching, John
Hayes, Thomas
Hill, John
Howard, William
Hunt, John
Hurd, Isaac
Howman, Joseph
Helman, Lacy
Howell, Jonathan
Halway, Byran
Hold, William

Helman, Thomas
Hall, Spence
Hill, James
Hayn, David
Haysford, William
Hill, James
Hall, Lyman
Hall, Nathan
Hughes, Thomas
Hubble, Thomas
Henry, Joseph
Hughes, John
Hemdy, Daniel
Halton, Moses
Hadson, Josiah
Hewit, Lewis
Hunter, Ezekiel
Hensby, John
Hubbard, Jacob
Hopkins, Christopher
Hoiste, Ephraim
Hubbel, Abel
Hughes, Thomas
Hilley, Edward
Hamsby, Thomas
Heath, Joseph
Hong, Simon
Hort, Ephraim
Hoites, Humphry
Harroon, Charles
Hammond, Charles
Holmes, Nathaniel
Hand, Thomas
Hand, William
Harden, Richard
Hooker, George
Harris, William
Harris, Nathaniel
Herrick, William
Hatch, Rubin
Hashton, Philip
Harding, Nathaniel
Holmes, Joseph
Hacker, Samuel
Hall, Moses
Heath, Charles
House, Enos
Howe, Edward
Hall, John
Henry, Butler

Henry, Michael
Heath, Seren
Hooper, Michael
Hensey, Patrick
Henry, Michael
Hatam, Benjamin
Hughes, Phelix
Hiss, Philip
Hughes, Greenroro
Holman, Henry
Hopkins, William
Hance, Henry
Hilliard, James
Harragall, William
House, Seren
Hamilton, Henry
Hicks, John
Harden, William
Hise, Nathaniel
Hooper, Sweet
Hawker, Edward
Huggand, Stephen
Harding, Frances
Hutchinson, Esau
Hodgkinson, Benjamin
Harner, Joseph
Hinley, William
Horns, Augustus
Hammer, Flint
Hobbs, William
Hancock, Samuel
Hawkin, John
Hicks, Benjamin
Harrington, Bartholomew
Hughes, Thomas
Hanwagan, James
Hopper, Edward
Hawcourt, Peter
Hart, John
Halley, Richard
Mendrick, Absolam
Ismay, George
Irvin, Michael
Indicot, Benjamin
Israel, Gosper
Ignacis, Joseph
Illiumbe, Ividesousis
Iqueritta, Philip
Izaguirre, Frances
Ireland, David

34

Duff, Daniel
Irwin, George
Irwin, Michael
Ireland, Joseph
Ingersall, Henry
Irons, James
Ireland, Joseph
Inguin. Joseph
Ingerson, John
Ingedon, Isaac
Isaacs, Isaac
Ingraham, John
Ingraham, Joseph
Ingersoll, Henry
Ireland, James
Ingraham, Joshua
Ivans, James
Irasetto, Joseph
Ingarsall, Joseph
Ivington, John
Johnston, John
Joyce, Samuel
Jones, John
Jenkin, David
Joyce, John
Justive, Simeon
Joamra, Vird
Jeune, Jermain
Joy, Samuel
Jackson, John
Joe ——
Jesbank, Abel
Jinks, Nathan
Justice, Samue
Jacen, Michael
Jask, Negro
Joel, Thomas
Jenks, William
Jowdant, Jean
Johnston, Robert
Jacobs, Joseph
Johnston, William
Jones, William
Johnson, Joseph
Jones, Richard
Jovelin, Govrad
Jackquin, James
Jones, Benjamin
Jones, Benjamin
Jatill, Francis

Joslite Willman
Jean, Clement
Jardin, Jean
Jacque, Guitne
Jacque, Guitmon
Johnston, William, 1
Johnston, William, 2
Jadan, Peter
Jean, Joseph
Jaque, Lewis
Jeffrey, James
Jackson, Henry
Jucba, Randon
Johnston, Paul
Jones, James
Jackson, John
Johnston, Miller
Johnston, Michael
Jones, Bial
Jeffries, John
Jones, Abraham
Jones, Samuel
Jackson, George
Johnson, William
Jordon, Nicholas
Jarnan, Francis
Johnson, Elias
Jones, Samuel
Jerun, Francis
Jucerria, Manuel Josh
Jones, William
Joie, John
Jones, Samuel
Job, Robert
Jones, Clayton
Johnson, Richard
Jeanesary, Benjamin
Jean, William
Jennings, William
Johnston, William, 1
Johnston, William, 2
Johnston, Edward
Jinks, Rufus
Joy, John
Jonas, Benjamin
James, John
Junus, Henry
Jones, William
James, John
Jones, John

Johnson, James
Jones, John
Johnson, James
Johnson, William
Jack, Black
Jack, John
Johnson, Samuel
Johnson, William
Jones, William
Jones, Benjamin
Jones, John
Jay, Jean
Jacob, Jean
Jenney. Langdon
Jengoux, Pierre
Josegsh, Mousa
Jouest, Antonio
Johnstone, James
Jorden, Jean
Jeffries, Joseph
Johnson, William
Johnson, Major
Johnson, James
Johnston, Simon
Jenny, Langholm
Jenny, John
Justus, Philip
Jones, Darl
Johnson, William, 1
Johnson, William, 2
Jones, Thomas, 1
Jones, Thomas, 2
Joseph, Antonio
Jemrey, George
Johnson, George
Joseph, Anthony
Juster, George
James, William
Jones, William
Jaikes, John
Jones, William
Jones, William
Jones, William
Jordan, Philip
Jassy, John
Jones, Alexander
Johnston, Robert
Joulet, Thomas
Johnston, George
Jones, John

Joseph. Thomas
Jamison, Daniel
Jones, William
Jones, Jacob
Johnston, Peter
Johnston, William
Jenkins, Solomon
Jeffries. Philip
Jeffers, Samuel
Johnson, John
Johnson, Francis
Jenny, Langhorn
Joy. Peter
Joy, Curtis
Johnston, William
Justus, George
Jones, William
Jones, John
Jones, Joseph
Joil, Thomas
Jenkins, Enoch
Jenkins, George
Jethsam, Oliver
Joy, Peter
Jennings, Nathaniel
Johnston, John
James, Reyan
Johnston, Robert
Jowelf, Thomas
Junus, Henry
Jenney, John
James, Benjamin
Jackson, Frederick
Junas, Henry
Jackson, Frederick
Jacobs, Wilson
Jacobs, Bella
Jacks, John
Jarvis, Edward
Jrangille, Jean Francis
Jeffers, Roswell
Johnston, William B.
Johnston, Stephen
Julian, Peter
Jordan, Peter
Jolt, Adam
Jones, Samuel
Jurdante, Jaques
Jourdant, Jean
Joaquire, Manuel

Jennings, William
Jones. John
Jack, John
Jenney, George
Jackson, James
Jordan, John
Jackson, Robert
Jowles, Thomas
Johnston, George
Jackson, Josiah
Johnson, John
Jaikson, Jonathan
Jeffers, William
Janes, Josiah
Jones, Jibb
Jarvis, Retuna
Jackson, George
Johnston, William
Johnston, Samuel
Johnston, Major
Johnston, Joseph
Jinny, Moses
Jones, Edward
Jackson, Frederick
Jeffries, Joseph
Jackson, Nathaniel
Jones, Ed
Jonan, ——
Johnston, Ebenezer
Jiles, Silas
Jennings, Thomas
Johnston, John
Joseph, Emanuel
Jeffries, Joseph
Joy, Josiah
Jackson Peter
Jacobus, Andrew
Johnson, Stephen
Keyborn, William
Kidd, John
Knowlton, William
Kelley, John, 1
Kelly, John, 2
King, William
Kelley, Michael
Kinne, Joseph
King, Joseph
Killis, Charles
Kenneday, William
Kidtona, Manuel

Knight, Thomas
Krowton, Ezekiel
Kelly, Seth
Kirkwood, James
Kirkwood, Thomas
Kiblano, Jean
Kitchen, Edward
Knox, John
Knowlton, Edward
Kenney, John
Kitler, John
Kelby, Samuel
King, Charles
King, Joseph
Kickson, James
Kinsland, Josiah
King, John
Kilby, John
Killer, Samuel
Kersey, William
Kelbey, Samuel
Kinney, Samuel
Kildair, Lewis
Kelley, William
Kirk, William
Kirby, Charles
Killenhouse, William
Kelley, Patrick
Kenneday, William
Knox, Jeremiah
Kale, Lewis
Killman, Gustavus
Ketcham, Samuel
Kenneday, Thomas, 1
Kenneday, Thomas, 2
King, Michael
Kennedy, David
King, John
Kenneday, Robert
Knapp, James
Keary, William
Kenneday, Robert
Knapp, Ebenezer
Kelley, Samuel
Kimberell, Nathaniel
Knight, Benjamin
Kane, John
Kellwan, Nehemiah
Kingburry, Nathaniel
King, Richard

Kain, John
King, Joseph
Kemplin, William
Kelley, John K., 1
Kean, Thomas
Kelley, John, 2
Kane, Edward
Kane, Barney
Kane, Patrick
Kelly, Hugh
Kirk, John
Kelley, John, 3
Kidd, George
Kenneday, Nathaniel
Keys, John
Keys, Anthony
Keys, Michael
Kidney, James
Knight, Benjamin
Keaton, Daniel
Kilts, John
Kilray, Daniel
Kelley, John, 4
King, Gilbert
King, Joseph
Knowles, James
Killen, Samuel
Kelter, Ogas
Kinwaird, William
Kensey, William
Kinsman, Benjamin
Kerril, John
Kingsley, William
Knowles, James
Kisler, Charles
Kenneday, Charles
Kelley, Oliver
Kelley, John
Kenim, Simon
Kelley, Abner
Kenneday, Jonathan
Kaddoody, Mark
Kelly, Timothy
King, John
Kelly, Roger
Keard, Nathaniel
Kennedy, James
Kelly, James
Knight, Ruben
Kelly, Abner

Keath, Tison
Kenyon, Elisha
King, John
Kersey, William
Kilbourn, Thomas
Kenney, John
Kilfundy, John
Ker, Jozon
Kenneday, James
Knowles, Nathaniel
Kelly, Abner
Ketcham, Edward
Kuthoopew, Frederick
Kane, Thomas
Knox, Seremiah
Knight, Thomas
Kenyon, Elisha
Kellry, Roy
Knight, Job
Kean, Sprague
Knowls, James
Knight, Thomas
Keller, John
Knight, Benjamin
Kyer, Louis
King, Jonathan
Kelley, Michael
Lucas, Lusian
Lillabridge, Jonathan
Linzey, Samuel
Linzey, William
Lowring, John
Letts, Ezekiel
Luckey, William
Lewis, Josiah
London, Richard
Laird, Thomas
Law, Ezekiel
Lee, Josiah
Leatherly, John
Le Caq, Philip
Le Vegne, Charles
Le Fargue, Louis
Le Poore, Joshua
Le Fougue, Alexander
Legro, Samuel
Lerandier, Pierre
L'Herox, Nicholas
Law, Ezekiel
Littlejohn, Thomas

Long, Frederick
Leary, Cornelius
Lawrence, Antonio
Lee, Peter
Lowery, John
Lambert, Richard
Lynn, Stephen
Lawrence, Samuel
Lamb, William
Little, Thomas
Lumbard, Peter
Lewis, Josiah
Leacks, William
Lapthorn, James
Linthorn, Richard
Lawrence, John
LeCose, William
Laura, Samuel
Lan Hubere, Francis
Lubard, Jacques
Lee, Stephen
Landon, George
Loney, Peter
Lasoca, Jachery
Loverin, William
Love, Thomas
Lawrence, Robert
Ludds, William
Loper, Emanuel
Lemons, Pierre
Leera, Joseph
Love, Stephen
Latham, Edward
Lattimer, Thomas
Livet, Thomas
Lavet, Daniel
Lee, Thomas
Lacon, Christopher
Legro, Joseph
Langler, John
Larkins, James
Langlord, Joseph
Langum, Franes
Larsolan, Lewis
Lincoln, Lewis
Lewis, Samuel
Lovett, James
Leech, John
Lefant, Jean
Lewis, Ellen

Lepach, Louis
Lafait, Anthony
Leblanc, Louis
Lelande, Jacob
Langola, Joseph
Lort, John
Lewis, Timothy, 1
Lewis, Timothy, 2
Low, William
Liar, Pierre
Lidman, John
Laighton, Samuel
Leafeat, John
Little, John
Lester, Christian
Little, Francis
Lewis, Charles
Layzer, Anthony
Lowe, James
Loreman, William
Leeme, Jack
Lowerry, Robert
Lenina, Joseph
Lizarn, Lienui
Lattain, Lorenzo
Luzard, Augustino
Lescimia, Joseph Pecanti
Lambuda, Thomas
Lambra, Cayettand
Lochare, Lones
Long, Enoch
Lyons, Archabold
Leech, James
Lane, William
Lattimer, William
Lowell, Israel
Lasker, Fred
Lee, Richard
Lawson, Joseph
Lee, John
Loran, Daniel
Lowell, Jonathan
Lowell, Abner, 1
Lowell, Abner, 2
Lovett, Thomas
Lowell, Jonathan
Lucas, James
Linn, Charles
Lefever, Samuel
Lines, Lamb

Lee, Richard
Lacope, Oliver
Lewis, John
Lasteo, Pierre
Lewis, Samuel
Lewis, James
Larbys, Charles
Lewis, John
Lenock, Tuft
Leech, Thomas
Lehman, George
Lack, John
La Coque, Guillman
Lemee, Rocque
Lake, Thomas
Luther, Nehemiah
Levnee, Rochue
Laley, Thomas
Lilliabridge, Thomas
Lillehorn, Joseph
Lord, Nathaniel
Lombard, Solomon
Leach, Thomas
Lasherty, John
Layton, Joseph
Lame, Evena
Ligond, Homer
Lupus, Loun
Leman, Jeremiah
Langer, Jonathan
Leach, Thomas
Lyons, Jonathan
Leyane, Jean Baptist
Levi, Nathaniel
Lapham, David
Lunt, Joseph
Lathrop, Elisha
Lathaop, Hezekiah
Lapthrop, Solomon
Lamb, David
Leechman, George
Lowering, John
Long, William
Lessley, John
Lewis, John
Law, Richard
Lafferty, Dennis
Lopez, Joseph
Lewis, Prisby
La Plan, Joseph

Langdon, Peter
Loggard, Patrick
Loveberry, John
Lightwell, John
Lay, Edward
Lee, Aaron
Lee, James
Lee, David
Leish, George
Layons, John
Long, Christian
Langdon, John
Lute, Philip
Leech, James
Logan, John
Langley, Thomas
Lenard, James
Lawrence, William
Lemon, Abraham
Legrange, Thomas
Laplairn, Bundirk
Lamt, Thomas
Laird, John
Little, John
Lowe, John
Lyle, Charles
Light, Louis
Lucker, William
Loring, Robert
Lovett, Thomas
Love, John
Lawrence, John
Lefevere, Nathaniel
Lee, Adam
Lane, William
Laborde, Fortune
Logoff, Eve
Latham James
Laird, John
Levett, Joseph
Lisby, Henry
Lewis, Daniel
Lyse, John
Latover, James
Luther, Rubin
Luther, Nehemiah
Lipp, Jessee
Leville, Peter
Lawton, Joseph
Limberick, John

Lunt, Joseph
Louis, David
Lynbick, Wittsby
Laird, Christopher
Leversey, John
Lunt, Joseph
Lemont, John
Lickeradan, Charles
Lyclar, Alexander
Lickerada, Charles
Lee, Thomas
Leonard, John
Leatherby, John
Lyons, Daniel
Lague, James
Love, John
Leverett, Thomas
Little, George
Lloyd, William
Lassan, David
Lichmond, George
Lewis, John
Leeraft, Benjamin
Leynock, John
Lewis, Andrew
Lee, Henry
Luder, Samuel
Lone, Adam
Larrick, Benjamin
Laborde, Frederick
Lefever, Samuel
Lewis, Samuel
Lascope, Julian
Lott, William
Lascope, Guillimot
Long, Jeremiah
Laird, Christopher
Layne, William
Lyon, Samuel
Lawrence, Samuel
Layton, Colsie
Lafever, Samuel
Lawrence, Samuel
Labone, Francois
Loring, Francis
Lunbrick, Francois
Latham, Thomas
Labordas, Demnar
Lewis, Samuel
Laggoff, Jeff

Lawrence, James
Lawrance, Thomas
Limburne, Christopher
Lewis, George
Laurency, John
Limburne, Christopher
Lumbardy, Peter
Lessington, John
Linva, Nicholas
Lawrie, John
Lewis, John
Little, John
Little, Philip
Lerong, Robert
Leach, Thomas
Lewis, Samuel
Lowerre, Robert
Lawrence, William
Lewis, Nathaniel
Lee, Thomas
Lynton, Joan
Lane, Thomas
Lee, Richard
Lunt, Skipper
Lilling, John
Lowett, Philip
Lyons, Ezekiel
London, John
Latham, David
Letts, Ezekiel
Land, Henry
Linot, Lewis
Lenard, Joseph
Lemosk, Powell
Lossett, Jean
Lepord, Piere
Lepord, Francis
Lilley, Almsted
Lakeman, Nathan
Lamere, Alexander
Lavonah, Michael
Le Rean, Jean
Lanvath, William
Lambert, Piere
Leach, Ezekiel
La Fille, Pierre
Lanal, Elnoque
Lewis, John
Laban, Basil
Laury, Homer

Lelande, Joseph
Le Girwin, Joseph
La Raison, Mathew
Laselieve, Joseph
Longue, Martin
Langolle, Andrew
Lamere, Alexander
Lenoze, Joseph
Lemee, John
Lozall, Pierre
Lloyd, James
Lally, Sampson
Lester, Henry
Lowerre, Jacob
Loraux, John
Lawbridge, Michael
Littleton, William
Le Porb, Piere
Lowden, Negro
Laroach, Gillian
Layfield, Lenolen
Lorton, Thomas
Lawrence, Joseph
Langley, Thomas
Lattimore, William
Langstaff, Thomas
Lyon, Peter
Lewis, Abraham
Lewis, Richard
Lake, Simon
Landman, Samuel
Lawrence, Michael
Lemot, John
Lalour, John
Lavigne, Pierre
Larada, Francis
Lewis, John
Lathrop, John
Lefen, Michael
Leviner, Joseph
Leford, Jean
Lindsley, Mathew
Lindsley, William
Lloyd, Simon
Lenham, John
Lanmand, Nicholas
Lyous, Michael
Ludwith, David
Leerce, Joseph

Lemonas, Peter	Lawrence, Isaac	McCann, Edward
Lameova, Michael	Lattimer, Peter	Moore, Abraham
Levanden, Anthony	Langley, Obadiah	Mason, James
Lameari, Jean	Legrange, Hezekiah	Malcom, John
Labog, Pierre	McKinsle, George	Martin, Michael
Larquan, Piere	Morton, James	Moore, Thomas
Lagarvet, Anthony	Morehouse, Abel	Martins, Martin
Lesteren, Lion	Maygahan, John	Murray, John
Law, Thomas	McCully, Caleb	Mathews, Richard
Landon, Peter	Markam, Elias	Maxwell, James
Larkin, Thomas	McCray, Gilbert	Maxwell, William
Leasear, John	Mathews, Josiah	Muller, Leonard
Lynch, Timothy	Maxwell, James	Mires, Koil
Lucie, Jean	McCray, John	McGill, James
Luyster, Benjamin	Merchant, Jean	Marcey, James
Lavea, Michael	McKeon, Thomas	Mariarty, Timothy
Langford, William	McKey, Patrick	McLaughlin, Peter
Langford, Darius	McKay, Patrick	Miller, Michael
Light, Samuel	McClesh, John	McGoggin, John
Lassly, Michael	Martin, Philip	Myers, Henry
La Casawyne, Michael	Morrell, Osborne	Murphy, John
Leach, William	McEvin, John	Marton, Oliver
Leonard, Simon	McDaniel, James	Mount, Richard
Law, John	Marshall, Thomas	Male, John
Lawrence, Thomas	Madding, John	Mullin, Robert
Lamie, Roque	Moore, Ralph	Morris, John
Laquise, Piere	Millen, Jacob	McDougall, William
Lewis, William	McKinsey, John	Morris, John
Lewis, Daniel	Martin, William	Myles, George
Lessell, John	Matson, James	Myatt, Jean
Lathmore, William	Mellens, Joseph	Mapson, Jean
Luckey, William	Moore, Wardman	Morgan, Abel
Lasken, William	McNeil, James	Martin, John
Lewis, Jesse	Miller, John	Murray, Charles
Lambert, Richard	Maxfield, Patrick	Martin, George
Lyons, Ephraim	Mite, David P.	Marshall, Thomas
Louis, Joseph	Murdock, James	Murdock, James
Lindsey, James	McNauch, John	Marle, Thomas
Lafferty, Dennis	Madding, John	Mills, William
Lindsay, Samuel	Mall, Enoch	Muller, Robert
Levzie, Bineva	Marting, Philip	Mortong, Philip
Lewis, John	McClure, William	Maskillin, Mathew
Lain, Peter	McArthur, John	Morton, James
Lowering, Samuel	Miller, Jacob	Malone, John
Laca, Anton	Maxwell, James	Mamford, Nathaniel
Lewis, Jesse	McDonald, Donald	McKellum, Mathew
Le Cour, Baptist	Montgomery, John	Maso, Jean
Landart, Stephen	McDaniel, James	Martin, Jesse
Lewis, John	McLaughlin, Philip	Moss, William
Lawson, Andrew	Moride, John	Munford, Richard

Morey, Jonathan
Mullet, Abraham
Main, William
Maxwell, William
McGill, Arthur
Mariner, John
Moulton, John
Moore, Joseph
Moore, Nathaniel
Matthias, Richard
Marral, Zachary
Miller, John
Martin, Daniel
Mildrid, George
Major, Simon
Morton, James
Morrell, Robert
McCarty, Andrew
Meritwal, Jean
Morare, Adam
Morey, Louis
Marney, David
Milchier, Jean
Montgomey, James
Maler, Francis
Marshall, Joseph
Mothe, Elikam
Miller, John
Merrell, John
Morton, George
McDonough, Patrick
McName, Francis
Martin, Jacok
Merchant, Jean
Meeck, Jacob
Manlose, Jacob
Montgomery, John
Migley, James
McNish, John
Morris, Robert
Mumford, Timothy
Mitchell, John
Manaford, Peter
Moflit, David
Mercy, Sylvester,
Murphy, Thomas
Martin, Lewis
McDaniel, John
Martin, Joseph'
McLain, Lewis

Murrow, David
Murrow, Samuel
Mariner, Hercules
Mainwright, Joseph
McDonald, Donald
McConnell, James
McKenney, James
Mills, John
McCanery, John
Montgomery, George
Mash, Thomas
Miles, Thomas
McCunn, Archibald
McGinnis, James
Manley, John
Moore, Thomas
Mulloy, Edward
Mangoose, George
Moore, Thomas
Mills, Francis
Mulloy, Francis
Malcom, Maurice
Merrick, Augustus
Morley, Joseph
Molose, Gilman
Molesan, Joseph
Manchester, Thadeus
Medcalf, Samuel
Marand, Auree
Merchant, Jean
Mercer, James
Mathews, Robert
Miles, John
Merrick, John
Mantsna, Joseph
Marmilla, Frances
Malong, Paul
Molla, Alexander
Miles, John
Mathamice, Pierre
Molton, George
McCrady, John
Miller, David
Morrell, Robert
Merrick, Samuel
Miller, Peter
Marse, Alexander
Moulton, George
McCormick, John
McCampsey, Mathew

Martin, Martin
Montague, Normand
Montague, William
Mix, Joseph
McCullock, William
Miller, William
Montgomery, George
McCallister, Patrick
McDonald, William
Montgomery, John
Morrell, John
Manda, Edward
Maxwell, James
Morgan, Henry
McClain, Francis
McGinness, Henry
Moore, James
Maxwell, John
Mires, Keile
Murray, Bryan
Murphy, Patrick
Moore, Thomas
McMichal, James
Motion, Enoch
Morris, Jonathan
Morgan, Thomas
McCloud, Peter
Moore, Thomas
Morton, Abner
Millbank, Robert
Morien, William
McCome, Paul
Mink, Burnet
Minks, John
Marran, William
Manhood, John
Mills, Andrew
McNeil, James
Martin, James
Moore, Adam
Mathews, Joseph
Murray, John
Merritt, John
Morris, John
Molton, Enoch
Mooton, John
Morton, Philip
Malsand, Thomas
Molloy, Silvanus
McHayan, William

McDonald, John
Moss, William
Mickevy, Roger
Mason, Stephen
Müllet, Leonard
Merchant, William
Mansfield, William
Martin, Damon
McGelpin, Andrew
Menlich, Jean Baptist
Menelich, John
Mersey, John
Mandeviniur, Jonathan
Montaire, Lewis
Miller, John James
Merchand, John
Manett, Etein
McCullem, Francis
McCrea, Roderick
Malcom, Lewis
Miles, Timothy
Mitchell, Benjamin
Merser, Clifton
Migile, Timothy
Money, Isaac
Mereff, Bistin
Mullin, William
Marsh, Edmund
Moody, Silas
Matre, Joseph
Mecury, Samuel
Moore, Henry
Melwin, George
Moses, Negro
Mans, Isaac
Morris, Daniel
Murray, Thomas
Mein, Springale
Maxwell, John
Messdone, William
Morgan, John
Mann, James
Millbown, James
Messell, Thomas
Millburn, Robert
Marbinnea, ——
Mamney, ——
Meneal, Lewis
Mahrin, Peter
McFarling, Bradford

Meyrick, Job
Moel, James
Marshland, Charles
Marcais, Etom
Malaque, Pierre
Martin, Gilowe
McIntire, Duncon
Mongender, Perrend
Moore, John
Moore, John
Moore, William
Maxwell, William
Morris, David
Mallory, Daniel
Mix, Elijah
Melch, William
Marston, Thomas
Morgan, John
McLane, Neil
Mutter, Ebenezer
Martin, Joseph
Meek, Timothy
Meak, John
Mansfield, Benjamin
McFarland, William
Mackneol, William
Meltward, Adam
McFarland, Daniel
Moore, William
Morselander, Sheren
Morselander, William
Meek, Joseph
May, John
Marsh, James
Mortimer, Benjamin
Mason, Augustus
McDonald, Alexander
Mathews, William
Merrick, Joseph
Morton, Abner
Morris, John
Manhee, John
Moree, W
Morton, Samuel
McCoy, Peter
Murray, John
Miller, John
Mannet, George
Merril, Nimrod
Miller, William

Martelns, Adam
McNeil, James
Maikser, Jean
Mathias, Robert
McFarling, James
McGee, John
Melwood, William
McKinsley, William
Moosey, Charles
Moore, Abraham
Martin, Peter
Morea, Gilmot
Massea, Charles
Mawdole, John
Millwood, John
Morley, James
Miller, John
McDaniel, James
May, George
McCormac, Hugh
Mortimore, Robert
McDonald, Petrie
McClarey, Daniel
McHenry, Barnaby
Morey, Lewis
Murray, William
McCape, Daniel
Malen, William
Mority, Edward
Morant, John
Martin, James
Munrow, Royal
Miller, Elijah
Morris, Ettsins
Morris, Philip
Mathewson, Thomas
Morrison, Murdock
Montgomery, James
Miller, George
Maxwell, David
Martine, Thomas
Mahlan, Stringe
Morse, Richard
Morgan, John
McWaters, Samuel
Murphy, Daniel
Mooney, Hugh
McDavid, John
McCloskey, Patrick
Marshall, John

McCormick, John
McCalpan, Walter
McKensie, John
Morrison, James
McClemens, Patrick
McLachlan, Benjamin
Martin, John
Martin, Thomas
McCulla, Patrick
Mascer, Andrew
McArthur, Charles
McClure, James
Matterga, William
Mariner, Hercules
Martin, Samuel
Mercer, Robert
McNeil, William
Mink, Renard
Myers, Peter
Mink, John
McGowen, James
Martin, Michael
Martin, Thomas
Metsard, Thomas
McIntire, Duncan
Merchant, Peter
Maples, Jonathan
Minow, Arnold
Mason, John
Mede, John
Mitchell, Anthony
Miller, Ebenezer
Mullin, Jonathan
May, John
Morris, John
Marshall, Benjamin
Morris, Andrew
Manars, Josiah
Meek, Abraham
Miles, Segar
Murphy, Thomas
McFarlan, Bradford
Maxwell, George
Muller, Jean
Morrice, Francis
Margabta, Jean
McCleaf, Henry
Mullent, Elime
Maneit, Pierre
Miller, Jonathan

Moucan, Francis
Moucan, Jean
Miller, Elijah
Marlgan, Jean
Munthbowk, Thomas
May, John
Mathews, William
Mills, John
McLaughlin, Philip
Mathews, John
Macay, John
Mackroy, Romulus
Maurice, James
Manchester, Silas
Manchester, John
Merry, John
Mann, Thomas
McGonegray, Robert
Millett, Thomas
Millett, Maurice
Morris, Thomas
McGee, John
Molny, John
Miller, Samuel
Murphy, John
Minniharm, Laurence
Monro, John
Mariner, John
Mathews, Richard
Motley, Alexander
Montgomery, James
Marian, Jean
Marian, Jean
Morana, Acri
Malcum, Maurice
Maston, James
Mulloy, Edward
Mathews, Robert
McGerr, James
McCowen, William
McLain, Edward
Martin, Simon
Martin, Daniel L.
Miller, Samuel
Martin, John
Martin, James
Martin, Embey
Munro, John
Mitchell, Joseph
Mix, Paul

Murrow, John
Mason, Halbert
McGandy, William
McDonough, Patrick
Mitchell, James
Martin, James
Martin, Nathaniel
Moss, John
Mason, Gerard B.
Messmong, George
Medcolf, John
Massey, James
McPherman, Malcolm
Murray, Daniel
McCash, John M.
Martin, Ananias
Morris, William
Mason, Louis
Moore, Thomas
Mercer, Robert
McCarty, Cornelius
McFall, James
Myers, Adam
Murria, Antonio
Marriott, James
Murria, Antonio
Moore, William
McDermott, William
McCullough, William
Muckleroy, Jacob
Muckleroy, Philip
Montgomery, George
Miners, Dirk
Murdock, John
Moore, William
Meecher, Usell
Martin, William
Murphy, Nicholas
Manlove, William
Marshall, Samuel
Monras, William
McCarty, William
Miller, Christopher
Mallett, John
Mathews, Jeffry
Ward, Francis
Murray, Daniel
Mitchell, Jean
Myers, Adam
McColtisler, Johnston

44

Moore, Samuel
Mariner, John
Moore, William
Monro, James
Martin, Francis
Murphy, Daniel
McCallister, Patrick
McClanegan, James
Newell, Amos
Nelson, Thomas
Nelson, Joseph
Northon, Daniel
Nandiva, Thomas
Nelson, William
Norris, Henry
Nourse, William
Noblat, Jean
Newbury, Elisha
Noves, Joseph
Northup, William
Northup, Harris
Negroe, Frank
Nelson, John
Newton, Adam
Nicholson, Alexander
Neville, Francis
Newhall, Joseph
Nichets, Martin
Newman, Thomas
Newton, Adam
Navey, Pierre
Nigley, James
Nurse, William
Noblet, John Mary
Newman, Thomas
Nigh, Gideon
Newtown, Adam
Newtown, William
Nelson, Andrew
Nicher, Thomas
Nelson, Thomas
Noble, James
Norton, John
Nicholson, Samuel
Navas, Francis,
Nichollson, George
Nash, Richard
Newman, Nathaniel
Newell, Nathaniel
Newall, Sucreason

Neville, Jean
Navall, Nathaniel
Norman, Peter
Nack, Dippen
Niester, John
Nicholls, James
Norfleet, John
Norman, John
Newille, Joseph
Norgand, Proper
Nutern, Pierre
Natalt, Jean
Negus, Thomas
Nocker, John
Negus, James
Newell, Andrew
Nathan, Joseph
Negis, John
Nixon, Robert
Nesbitt, Thomas
Negbel, Joseph
Neglee, James
Nore, William
Nelson, Alexander
Nathay, John
Nathay, John
Norton, Nicholas
Negg, Michael
Nich, Richard
Nicholas, Richard
Norton, John
Newton, Adam
Noblet, Mary John
Norton, Jacob
Norva, Jaque, 1
Norva, Jaque, 2
Necar, Gideon
Nandus, Hosea
Nelson, Alexander
Norton, Peter
Norton, Elijah
Newcomb, Andrew
Norman, Joseph
Newman, Thomas
Neating, Ebenezer
Nicholson, William
Newman, Moses
Newman, Thomas
Nicholls, George
Nicholls, Richard

Nealson, William
Noble, Arnox
North, Anfield
Nailer, Archibald
Nutter, David
Nutter, Joseph
Newton, William
Norton, William
Newton, John
Newarb, William
Nichols, James
Newgal, Nicholas
Nichols, John
Navane, Simon
Noel, William
Nicks, George
Nabb, Ebenezer
Nyles, Robert
Niles, Frank
Nuttin, John
Nestora, Bartholomew
Nicholls, Allen
Neilson, Alexander
Newall, Ebenezer
Neal, George
Normay, Joseph
Newman, Samuel
Neilson, Abraham
Neilson, James
Neville, Michael
Newman, Frances
Nicholson, Thomas
Norton, John
Nelson, John
Neilson, Joseph
Norman, James
Newell, Joseph
Newcomb, John
Norie, John
Neal, David
Nathan, Benjamin
Neal, David
Nicholson, George
Norton, Peter
Negroe, James
Newell, Robert
Nutting, Ebenezer
Nowell, Nathaniel
Nightingale, William
Ogee, Pierrie

Oliver, George
Oswald, Henry
Owens, John
Otter, Benjamin
Oubler, John
Oat, Israel
Osborne, Joseph
O'Brien, John
Ousanan, Charles
Owen, John
Ovett, Samuel
Otis, William
Onsware, Ebenezer
Oakley, Solomon
Owens, Anthony
Oseglass, John
Othes, Gregorian
O'Bryen, William
Onsey, Samuel
Onsey, William
Obey, John, 1
Obey, John, 2
Oliver, Anthony
Oshire, Jean
Olive' Don R. Antonio
Olazo, Devo
Olarra, Raymond D.
O'Brien, Edward
Owens, Samuel
Orgall, John
Owal, Lewis
Ovans, Jonathan
Ormunde, Edward
Outon, Jay
Oliver, James
O'Hara, Patrick
O'Neil, John
Oldsmith, John
Owens, Archibald
O'Hara, Patrick
Orsley, Patrick
Ord, Allen
Oates, Joseph
O'Brien, Cornelius
Oshire, Lewis
Oshire, Gabriel
Oates, Isaac
Oliver, Zebulon
Obourn, Daniel
Orseat, Emanuel

Orman, Sebastian
Olbro, Daniel
Osgood, John
Oakford, Charles
Osborn, John
Ogner, Richard
Orrock, John
O'Neil, John
Overatt, Vincent
Otini, Andre
Oliver, James
Oliver, James
Orr, William
Osman, John
Outon J.
Owens, Barnick
Odiron, Samuel
Oderon, Samuel
Ovington, Samuel
Oakman, John
Owens, James
Oldham, George
Ord, John
Ohara, Robert
Osena, Stephen
O'Harra, Patrick
Outton, John
Otis, Samuel
Otine, Andre
Oliver, James
Ogilong, John
Oliver, James
Prince, Benjamin
Pollard, John
Peters, John
Posture, Edward
Pease, Elisha
Perry, Raymond
Perry, William
Peals, William
Pierol, Jeremiah
Parker, John
Pribble, Edward
Palmer, George
Peters, Francis
Putman, Creece
Parker, Luther
Parker, John
Pollin, Jonathan
Pierre, Jean

Palmer, William
Port, Anthony
Pipon, Henry
Palmer, Jonas
Price, Reoson
Peck, Andrew
Priston, Nicholas
Parker, Samuel
Parker, Thadeus
Pass, Richard
Paddock, Joseph
Paddock, Abell
Paddock, Silas
Porter, Thomas
Palmer, William
Pettis, Ephraim
Price, Samuel
Perkins, William
Parker, Thadeus
Pearsol, Edward
Poole, John
Platte, John
Porter, David
Parsons, William
Parshal, Francis
Person, Manuel
Pullet, James
Plachores, Nathaniel
Pelonene, Jaque
Poole, Richard
Pettis, Nathan
Poble, Mathew
Pelvert, John
Palicutt, John
Payne, Thomas
Poore, Joseph
Payne, John
Purnell, William
Pamphillion, Nicholas
Parker, George
Potter, Ephraim
Peade, Edward
Patterson, William
Pell, Samuel
Paschal, Edmond
Poloske, Elbani
Porter, David
Parsons, Joseph
Prentis, Stanton
Perkins, Joseph

46

Palmer, Philip
Poore, William
Proctor, Joseph
Peck, Andrew
Park, George
Porter, David
Proud, John
Proud, Joseph
Presson, Isaac
Prate, Benjamin
Perinell, Charles
Pierce, Richard
Ploughman, John
Pitman, Jonathan
Peacock, John
Price, Edward
Pemberton, Amos
Pratt, Ezra
Pendleton, John
Pemberton, William
Pitkins, Seli
Primm, Henry
Pinkeman, Robert
Parks, George
Pribble, John
Patterson, Peter
Powell, John
Peterson, Joseph
Peterkin, John
Perry, William
Perora, Peter
Perons, Peter
Parsons, William
Purlett, Peter
Paschall, Leroy
Palto, Peter
Pike, Amos
Parke, George L.
Parker, John
Putman, Abraham
Presson, Andrew
Provost, Claud
Philip, Piere
Palmer, Mathew
Planne, Piere
Parde, Joseph
Permanouf, Antoni
Philip, Joseph
Phipise, Joseph
Pitman, Jonathan

Palmer, James
Pursell, Edward
Pound, Silvester
Patridge, David
Parkens, Joseph
Pinkel, Charles
Poke, William
Prentiss, Nathaniel
Porter, Samuel
Patch, Israel
Porter, Frederic
Parsons, Stephen
Pribble, John
Poore, Morris
Powder, William
Patterson, John
Patterson, John
Pierce, Stephen
Pierson, Joseph
Porter, Edward
Proctor, James
Porter, Charles
Payatt, Piere
Pittman, John
Payne, William
Pett, William
Peck, Simon
Prentiss, Robert
Paltd, Peter
Parsons, James
Price, Reoson
Philips, Samuel
Poges, Daniel
Pine, James
Perkin, Jonathan
Parker, John
Porter, Charles
Peomond, Jean Baptist
Parnell, Thomas
Parks, Richard
Polse, Samuel
Polse, William
Parker, Edward
Pierce, Richard
Penfield, Nathaniel
Plumstead, John
Paul, William
Pepper, Michael
Phillips, John
Pierre, Jessee

Priel, William
Parsons, James
Pelricay Gotodi
Parker, Luther
Pollard, Peter
Perry, William
Poole, David
Peaher, Samuel
Powell, Thomas
Posture, Thomas
Perry, Ramin
Pedlock, Edward
Parker, George
Parker, Samuel
Payton, William
Palmer, William
Palmer, Joshua
Palmer, Gay
Perkins, Jaben
Punham, Ephraim
Pimelton, Simeon
Pimelton, John
Pontesty, Joseph
Pegit, Jean
Parrie, Gabriel
Parol, Jean
Parsons, Joseph
Poinchet, Michael
Pisung, Jean
Portois, Frank
Pogsin, Salvardo
Peddlefoot, Zachary
Phillips, John
Proud, John
Potter, Charles
Peckworth, John
Peck, William
Padick, Daniel
Parsons, Jeremiah
Plunnett, Elten
Packet, Jean
Plumer, James
Peck, Andrew
Peterson, Hance
Peterson, Ebenezer
Parsons, James
Peckham, Gardner
Petre, James
Punce, Piere
Pendleton, Sylvester

Pond, Charles
Pond, Peter
Pitman, John
Philbrook, Thomas
Pezes, Joseph Antonio
Picko, Juan
Pontar, Hosea
Pardindes, Christo
Parpot, Dominick
Poirant, Gulman
Pechin, Gulial
Peal, Benjamin
Poland, John
Parsons, John
Pedgore, Solomon
Perry, Joseph
Poni, Gulman
Plenty, Franes
Pelit, Pierre
Pion, Augustus
Pitchcock, Elas
Picolet, Piere
Ponsard, Frances
Parsons, Samuel
Perall, Thomas
Palmer, John
Prince (negro)
Pescod, George
Pill, George
Pope, Alexander
Pervis, Jabez
Picher, Jean
Pelle, Sabastian
Peck, Joseph
Phillips, Edward
Penwell, James
Poole, Robert
Peril, James
Partidge, James
Power, Patrick
Poullain, Jean
Parlot, Joseph
Postian, Jean
Palmer, Lemuel
Payne, Josiah
Plumckett, Thomas
Pelit, John
Peck, Joseph
Pinkman, Jonathan
Prought, Joseph

Perry, John
Pillian, Joseph
Plemate, William
Prettryman, Benjamin
Prince, Charles
Payne, Oliver
Pearce, Jonathan
Pease, Estrant
Philips, John
Poor, Thomas
Palmer, Alisha
Peose, Alphred
Powers, Richard
Porter, Charles
Pegee, Jean
Prichard, John
Peshire, Jean
Plannett, Ettena
Padonan, Journey
Pratt, Ebenezer
Pettis, Daniel
Phimmer, James
Palmer, William
Pindar, William
Pierce, Benjamin
Payne, James
Peck, James
Pees, Alexander
Pees, John
Potter, Rufus
Philips, Nathan
Pitcher, James
Peck, Joseph
Panks, Anthony
Pearce, John
Palot, Moses
Parker, Peter
Parish, John
Parker, Ebenezer
Price, Edward
Porter, William
Preno, Andre
Pouchett, Mark
Porlace, Eatenia
Perien, Peter
Patterson, William
Philips, Thomas
Pecke, Benjamin
Pardley, Jacob
Pitman, George

Price, Richard
Peters, John
Phippin, Thomas
Poore, Henry
Phippin, Nathaniel
Powell, Thomas
Philip, Lewis
Piere, Antonio
Payne, William
Pegget, Silas
Pendleton, Sylvester
Patterson, Hance
Peterson, Aaron
Parker, Timothy
Post, Jeremiah
Poole, Hosea
Pratt, Ezra
Pike, John
Pride, Jonathan
Pond, Pennell
Palmer, Moses
Perry, William
Porter, Howard
Porter John
Park, Thomas
Patterson, W.
Porter, John
Patterson, Edward
Penoy, Peter
Pitt, Thomas
Price, Nathaniel
Parsons, William
Philip, John
Pearce, Benjamin
Philip, John
Pope, John
Parkson, Thomas
Powell, Richard
Perry, William
Pihto, Isaac
Pierre, Jean
Parong, Sebastian
Pue, Lewis De
Pogan, Henry
Pitts, W.
Pool, Robert
Pemberton, Thomas
Painter, Jacob
Provott, Paul
Perry, Richard

Poor, Morris
Pear, John
Power, Stephen
Price, Joseph
Porson, Nathaniel
Prate, James
Parkard, John
Patrick, Joseph
Poteer, Thomas
Porter, John
Peront, Piere
Pettit, Isaac
Pain, B.
Parker, Amos
Primus, Edward
Poseter, Seren
Primus, Edward
Price, William
Pearce, Amos
Panier, Emea
Paseau, Roman
Pirre, Incali
Pearson, John
Painter, Jacob
Prande, Nicholas, 1
Prande, Nicholas, 2
Perry, William
Parker, Amos
Palmer, Daniel
Pillsbury, Truston
Potter, Abijah
Proby, James
Proctor, Samuel
Payne, Thomas
Quelgrise, Lewis
Quinch, James
Quigg, Duncan
Quigg, Duncan
Quinn, Samuel
Quand, Thomas
Quality, Joseph
Quonier, Samuel
Quality, Josiah
Quality, James
Quality, James
Quality, James
Quiot, Charles
Quamer, Samuel
Reno, Frederick
Rogua, Francis

Randall, William
Ribble, George
Rush, Daniel
Richards, William
Rant, James
Randell, Joseph
Ross, Daniel
Reynelds, Thomas
Ray, Nathaniel
Rockwood, Elisha
Rogers, John
Roulong, Charles
Royster, John
Regan, Julian
Rackalong, Antonio
Rich, Elisha
Randal, Dolly
Richman, Ebenezer
Randol, Nathaniel
Rathbun, Roger
Randall, Nathaniel
Reed, John
Riker, Henry
Robins, Enoch
Rice, Nathaniel
Reed, Jonathan
Roberts, James
Ridgeway, John
Rawson, Francis
Raymons, William
Robertson, Elisha
Ross, Andrew
Ross, John
Robert, Julian
Richards, Oliver
Robert, John
Recour, Lewis
Ryan, Peter
Read, Benjamin
Richard, Benjamin
Robertson, John
Rennick, Thomas
Raye, Nathaniel
Rothburn, Samuel
Reed, William
Rogers, Thomas
Rice, John
Rozis, Lawrence
Richards, Gilbert
River, Joseph

Richmond, Seth
Rathburn, Samuel
Redick, Edward
Rowley, John
Rver, Piere
Rozea, Blost
Rockway, John
Rose, Prosper
Rockwell, Jabez
Rude, Ezekiel
Randall, Nathaniel
Rogers, John
Reynolds, Thomas
Rhodes, Silvester
Ross, George
Rice, James
Reed, Levi
Ross, William
Roberts, William
Rowen, George
Rodgers, James
Roberts, James
Roso, William
Ross, Thomas
Rice, Edward
Rice, Noah
Rice, William
Robertson, Charles
Robertson, James
Roberts, James
Rowley, Sliter
Ramlies, Peter
Reuben, Levi
Reed, Jeremiah
Royster, Richard
Robertson, Jeremiah
Ribble, George
Roush, Daniel
Richards, William
Rant, James
Randell, Joseph
Rogers, Emanuel
Reed, Eliphas
Rawson, Arthur
Romolus, Benjamin
Round, Nathaniel
Rose, John
Riker, Henry
Robertson, John
Rogers, John

Robins, James
Rose, Gideon
Rice, John
Rogers, Nicholas
Randell, Paul
Randell, Joses
Reed, John
Russell, Samuel
Rilly, Philip
Round, Nathaniel
Rawson, Arthur
Russell, Valentine
Ronder, Lewis
Rewof, Louis
Roget, Joseph
Rodrigo, Francis
Rano, Jean Baptist
Rodent, Jean Baptist
Refitter, Jaques
Rouges, Jean Baptist
Ricker, Henry
Robins, Enoch
Rathburn, Peter
Robertson, Thomas
Rogers, Thomas
Ropper, Bartrim
Romary, Petre
Ross, Peter
Randall, William
Roulong, Charles
Ruddock, Eden
Rust, William
Richmond, Benjamin
Rider, Lewis
Reed, William
Roas, William
Rogers, John
Reynolds, Thomas
Robertson, George
Rogers, John
Randall, Edward
Rigo, Joseph
Rowland Patrick
Robertson, Charles
Ross, James
Rowley, John
Riley, Philip
Robertson, John
River, John
Riley, James

Rothers, Benjamin
Richards, James
Rogue, John Francis
Ruth, John
Rogers, George
Riker, R.
Richmond, Seth
Reynolds, Richard
Redman, Benjamin
Roach, Lawrence
Roke, John
Rosca, Jean
Round, John
Richmond, Seth
Roth, John
Randall, Thomas
Round, Samuel
Ross, William
Robertson, John
Rose, Philip
Richman, Cussing
Robins, Enoch
Rathbun, Norman
Rathburne, Rogers
Rossean, Augustus
Russell, Jonathan
Rust William
Rogers, Paul
Ritch, Ebenezer
Richardson, Pierre
Renean, Jean
Reynolds, Nathaniel
Rust, John
Rigmorse, James
Ryon, Renee
Rossean, Gulem
Renand, Louis
Ringurd, Pierre
Robinson, Nathaniel
Reid, Hugh
Rollin, Toby
Rogert, John
Renear, Pierre
Renovil, Jean
Rotesla, Bostion
Russell, James
Richardson, William
Randall, Charles
Reynolds, John
Roger, Robert

Rodien, Michael
Requal, Jean
Robinson, Anthony
Rowe, William
Robinson, Jehew
Rone, Jack
Rion, John
Renee, Thomas
Robertson, Samuel
Rogers, Ebenezer
Raymond, Janes
Reed, Andre
Russell, Pierre
Red, John
Randles, George
Robinson, Ebenezer
Rester, Jessee
Richards, John
Roach, Joseph
Rube, Ebenezer
Rowe, John
Robertson, James
Riordan, Daniel
Ripley, Rambell
Robinson, Mark
Richardson, David
Ross, Melong
Rowsery, William
Robbinson, Thomas
Ross, Archibald
Robinson, David
Roberts, Samuel
Roen, Jacque
Robbins, James
Reo, Jean
Randall, Benjamin
Right, Jacob
Ross, John Stone
Rose, Samuel
Ryan, Frank
Ran, Jean C.
Round, Hampton
Riddler, Isaac, 1
Ridler, Isaac, 2
Ryan, Thomas
Raiden, Daniel
Reeves, Thomas
Robert, Arthur
Rosanet, Jean Baptist
Runyan, Joseph

Renan, Jean Nosta
Ridge, John
Roberts, Edward
Russell, William
Robinson, Thomas
Ripley, Paul
Rivers, Thomas
Rivers, Paul
Rezzick, Thomas
Rambert, John
Ross, George
Ruban, Peter
Robinson, John
Ruffie, Lewey
Randall, Charles
Ross, William
Rainham, Richard
Reade, Oliver
Robinson, Joseph
Randall, Joseph
Robertson, Joseph
Romeria, Deigo
Rayoor, Jean
Robinson, John
Ruff, John
Russell, Edward
Robinson, John
Reeves, Thomas
Ridley, Thomas
Roberts, Aaron
Rich, Freeman
Rogers, Dudson
Richard, Benjamin
Rattan, Peter
Ridley, Amos
Rouse, Andrew
Rouse, Claud
Rupper, John
Rogers, John
Riders, John
Rumsower, Henry
Reiton, Jacob
Robb, Thomas
Rowing, George
Rubin, Thomas
Reed, Christian
Reed, Thomas
Round, Thomas
Rutley, Pompy
Randall, Joseph

Rawson, James
Reed, George
Repent, Barton
Rice, James
Rafferty, Patrick
Robins, Daniel
Reed, Curtis
Reed, Barnard
Rainiot, Thomas
Roberts, James
Roderick, Anthony
Roberts, William
Roberts, Joseph
Redfield, James
Rich, Mathew
Rich, Nathan
Ranshaw, Benjamin
Reynolds, Richard
Ricker, Clement
Raingul, Michael
Robinson, William
Reen, Nicholas
Rickman, Nathaniel
Richards, Pierre
Roberts, William
Robertson, John
Rice, John
Ribas, Thomas De
Rogeas, Franco
Ray, Alexander
Rogers, William
Ropeley, Paul
Reef, John
Rivington, John
Roman, Francis
Rawson, James
Roberts, Moses
Ridden, Lewis
Ross, David
Ross, Daniel
Renow, Michael
Remong, Jean
Rockwell, Daniel
Rowson, James
Ruper, Nathaniel
Rice, John
Ross, Daniel
Rose, John
Royster, John
Rickett, John

Ray, John
Reed, Joseph
Rouge, Jean James
Rollin, John
Robertson, Esa
Rieve, Daniel
Richardson, John
Race, Thomas
Ramsdale, Joseph
Reed, Job
Raymond, George
Ryan, Michael
Russell, Jacob
Rice, Benjamin
Ross, Thomas
Randall, Jesse
Rogue, Jean
Reardan, Jeremiah
Robins, William
Roberts, Epaparas
Royen, Augustus
Rieves, Israel
Roberts, Aaron
Roberts, William
Robinson, James
Ruse, Daniel
Robinson, James
Ramsden, Abner
Roberts, Moses
Robehaird, James
Raymond, William
Rose, Gideon
Rarrham, Richard
Rowlin, John Frederick
Ryan, Jacob
Reynolds, Elisha
Robertson, Ebenezer
Robertson, James
Richards, Diah
Ruth, John
Sepolo, Leonard
Smith, Jonathan
Slewman, Thomas
Saddler, George
Satchell, Jonothan
Sloakim, Christopher
Smith, Henry
Sawyer, Ephraim
Sweet, Godfrey
Stoddard, Thomas

Slikes, Josiah
Shaw, Samuel
Sealey, Thomas
Stewart, Samuel
Stewart, John
Simons, Francis
Stewart, Jabez
Surado, Andre
Sasset, Juan
Smith, Samuel
Smith, James
Smith, Rockwell
Smith, Thomas
Sampson, Stephen
Sturtivard, John
Stone, Elijah
Sayers, Joseph
Sawyer, John
Sherburn, Thomas
Sntervant, John
Spring, Charles
Shepherd, John
Smith, David
Snyder, Jacob
Spratt, Philip
Skinner, Richard
Shappell, La
Smith, Samuel
Sutterwis, Lewis John
Silver, Francis
Seaton, George
Simmons, Hildoves
Shepherd, James
Stott, Jonathan
Slade, Benjamin
Sawyer, Ephraim
Smith, Jonathan
Stanton, Nathaniel
Sterry, William
Smith, Daniel
Stanton, John
Stockwell, Simeon
Scudder, David
Shaw, Samuel
Sheffield, John
Subbs, Benjamin
Satton, Joseph
Swate, Absolem
Sherman, John
Scott, Thomas

Stephens, John
Salmishall, Gilbert
Stevens, William
Smiley, William
Suldon, Myles
Schelderope, Milchion
Sheridan, John
Smith, James
Spier, John
Stephenson, John
Shiffin, George
Steele, Thomas
Shoakley, Joseph
Stanley, William
Slyde, Samuel
Stephens, William
Seeley, Thomas
Smith, Joseph
Sweeting, Nathaniel
Swapple, Thomas
Stones, Job
Smith, David
Stiles, Josiah
Shockley, Joseph
Slaughter, Mathew
Stanley, William
Shindle, Jacob
Simmons, Paul
Stouts, John
Summers, George
Smith, Archilles
Shewen, John
Simpson, Benjamin
Simpson, Thomas
Smith, Daniel
Smith, Benjamin
Shepherd, James
Snellin, John
Sondower, Christian
Sergeant, Thomas
Smith, Martin
Straud, Joseph
Stewart, Thomas
Spear, Robert
Stephenson, David
Smith, William
Stocy, Nathaniel
Sherman, Samuel
Stone, William
Smith, Roger

Stephens, William
Stubbs, Benjamin
Sawyer, William
Sawyer, Peter
Salter, Thomas
Short, Joseph
Stewart, Edward
Stedham, Daniel
Soul, Moses
Sloan, Edward
Shopley, Daniel
Spicewood, Lancaster
Sasson, David
Stewart, Daniel
Smith, Anthony
Stearns, John
Steward, Elijah
Scott, John
Smith, Alexander
Scull, Mitchell
Stephens, Henry
Smith, Epaphras
Simons, Nero
Smith, Samuel
Sweeney, John
Stone, Thomas
Sunderland, Edward
Sathele, John
Stoddart, Thomas
Stoddard, Israel
Shoakley, Joseph
Stewart, Jabez
Strange, James
Shaddon, John
Sweet, Godpede
Slade, Benjamin
Sloates, Andrew
Smith, Joseph
Sego, Jean Baptist
Smith, Haymond
Simmons, Richard
Smith, Joseph
Smith, Thomas
Stout, Daniel
Sawyer, Ephraim
Sawyer, Jeremiah
Salter, Thomas
Sawyer, Benjamin
Shaw, Samuel
Sproat, Alexander

Saddler, George
Smith, John
Shaw, Joseph
Smith, Daniel
Seeley, Thomas
Sherburne, Benjamin
Simonds, Francis
Smith, Thomas
Stanford, Richard
Stouts, Andrew
Sproat, Alexander
Smith, Andrew
Slae, David
Sullivan, Dennis
Simmonds, Peter
Scott, Robert
Sachell, Jonathan
Sachell, John
Shamron, Patrick
Smith, William
Stroud, Joseph
Scott, Christopher
Sweeney, John
Stanley, William
Stiles, Joshua
Surf, Jack C.
Sheridan, James
Starks, Benjamin
Simonds, Jeremiah
Stillwell, Enoch
Sprague Simon
Stoddard, Noah
Secraft, Benjamin
Smothers, Peter
Stagger, Conrad
Swery, Daniel
Surrondo, Francis
Swayne, James
Spencer, Nicholas
Sisson, Gilbert
Smith, Thomas
Stikes, John
Shoemaker, James
Skinner, Samuel
Sendder, David
Sampson, Stephen
Sherer, Gilbert
Stocker, Hugh
Stocker, William
Sunderland, Edwin

Stannard, William
Shappo, Mathew
Stevens, John
Smith, Thomas
Same, Edward
Stephen, John
Shiner, Frederick
Smith, Clement
Spier, John
Swellings, Joshua
Sablong, Francisco
Sadden, George
Smith, Archibald
Shokloy, Samuel
Sumner, Rufus
Share, Elisha
Smallpiece, Robert
Shafe, John
Stoneford, Boston
Stone, Thomas
Sellers, Edward
Seager, George
Shambo, Mathew
Shirkley, John
Sheans, Brittle
Spicer, John
Sullivan, Thomas
Sunderland, Edward
Stacy, Thomas
Slight, Joseph
Shampore, Mathew
Solomon, Thomas
Shiner, Frederick
Stoddart, Israel
Smith, David
Stone, Thomas
Sarfe, Peter
Sherman, Samuel
Small, Hicks
Smith, Thomas
Stilwell, Enoch
Stiles, John
St. Domingo, Francis
Skay, John
Shaw, James
Shibley, Jacob
Slide, Samuel
Salisbury, Luther
Sunderland, Amos
Shepherd, John

Smith, Thomas
Sharke, Robert
Smith, Abraham
Singer, John
Sauce, Edward
Staggar, Conrad
Spencer, Thomas
Salter, John
Sentalier, Abraham
Sergeant, Francis
St. Thomas, John
Smith, Daniel
Stanford, Butler
Scranton, William
Smith, James
Scope, Julian
Smith, Roger
Stiger, John
Stagger, Edward
Spicer, John
Smith, Clemont
Sawyer, James
Shaw, James
Schwoob, Peter
Shroak, Jacob
Stanley, Peter
Steham, John
Surtes, Hugh
Sweat, Enoch
St. Clair, John
Stone, Amos
Seabury, Lamb
Spry, Gideon
Sharpley, Joseph
Stober, Jacob
Saint, John
Sharpe, Peter
Snabilty, James
Shepherd, John
Stilwell, John
Sharpley, John
Spinks, John
Steward, Samuel
Sullivan, Patrick
Shaw, Jeremiah
Spikeman, Richard
Sawyer, Daniel
Spriggs, John
Simmons, John
Sammian, Jacob

Stanhope, John
Sanders, Henry
Spice, Henry
Staaggers, John
Shurman, Thomas
Simmonds, John
Swean, Peter
Sheilow, Nicholas
Saldat, Ellena
Salmon, John
Shepherd, Robert
Space, Henry
Sparrows, James
Sevithith, Otis
Singer, John
Scott, James
Spencer, Thomas
Simons, Champion
Stone, Thomas
Springer, Richard
Sherman, Samuel
Stacey, Thomas
Shaw, Daniel
Stone, Thomas
Stredges, Samuel
Starkweather, Woodbury
Stoney, Mathew
Smith, Thomas
Sprigg, John
Stringer, John
Service, William
Snow, Sylvanus
Smith, Jack
Smith, William
Sand, Charles
Smithson, Thomas
Sampson, Joseph
Spriggs, Joshua
Stedham, Daniel
Smith, John
Smith, Benjamin
Smith, John
Smith, Charles
Smith, Basil
Smith, Busken
Stone, Richard
Stone, Donald
Sole, Assia
Sluddard, Henry
Stutson, Smith

Stoddart, Edward, 1
Spooner, David
Santis, Anthony
Steelman, James
Spooner, Caleb
Shearman, Henry
Shearman, Stephen
Snow, Seth
Shadere, Conklin
Saterly, William
Sitchell, John
Stoddart, Edward, 2
Smith, John
Steer, John
Saunders, John
Standard, Lemdol
Stearny, William
Stevenson, Robert
Sherre, Andrew
Stone, Samuel
Stanton, Nathaniel
Smith, John
Smith, Jasper
Stalkweather, Samuel
Smith, John
Shelton, Benjamin
Setchell, Jonathan
Spriggs, Thomas
Smith, Zebediah
Stanton, Daniel
Scott, John
Slarick, Jean Louis
Sharper, Philip
Sweet, Benjamin
Slane, John
Shearman, Gideon
Sarde, Louis
Sallabie, Michael
Smith, Andrew
Stoker, John
Savage, Belias
Silvester, Manuel
Southwood, John
Sloan, Timothy
Slager, Thomas
Sutton, Thomas
Smight, John
Sawyer, Thomas
Smith, James
Spear, James

Sutton, George
Smart, Peter
Smith, John
Strong, Edmond
Swift, Martin
Sampson, John
Smack, William
Snider, William
Slough, Thomas
Smith, Eliezer
Sarbett, Thomas
Shilling, Jack
Simpkins, William
Smith, Richard
Shaw, Thomas
Savage, Allen
Sloeman, Andrew
Scott, John
Sutton, James
Soward, Charles
Shea, Patrick
Slowell, Isaac
Shebzain, Philip
Summers, John
Scott, William
Smith, Richard
Snider, Peter
Saunders, Daniel
Smith, Ezekiel
Simmons, David
Star, Timothy
Shaw, William
Shane, Thomas
Strand, Joseph
Savage, Nathaniel
Sago, Abraham
Simons, Boswell
Simmons, Chapman
Smith, Easoph
Sherns, Andrew
Shean, Jean
Stanford, Robert
Shad, Solomon
Smith, John
Stubbley, John
Smith, Laban
Stephens, Benjamin
Smith, Richard
Spencer, James
Stilwell, Nicholas

Shute, Enoch
Smith, Joseph
Swift, Thomas
Smith, James
Steward, Lewis
Stott, Seren
Siekes, Richard
Sadens, John
Speck, Eliphes
Seratte, Francis
Stevens, Levert
Sussell, John
Scott, John
Suret, Godfrey
Stevens, James
Selvina, Antony
Smith, Edward
Stone, Richard
Stone, Abeny
Scees, Henry
Suttegraz, Franco Deo
Suffearraire, Jaqueio
Sugastta, Manuel
Sandoval, Manuel
Sunoueaux, Franco
Sogne, Raimond
Shatille, Joseph
Smallwood, John
Smalwood, Thomas
Stewart, Robert
Shepherd, Robert
Swire, William
Smith, Stephen
Shout, Enoch
Speakl, Martin
Stephens, William
Slee, John
Smith, John
Sentelume, Adam
Speake, John
Stringer, John
Scott, George
Simons, Nathaniel
Seager, Adam
Simmons, John
Senior, John
Spencer, Joseph
Serles, Joel
Shaw, Abner
Spaner, Joshua

Smith, Sullivan
Swean, Peter
Smith, James
Salmon, John
Spellman, William
Shovong, Christopher
Stratia, Josna Bla
Shatalier, Joseph
Snyker, Roman
Suneneau, Francis
Suneneaw, John
Stapler, Abijah
Shetlene, George
Smith, Jebediah
Savage, Nathaniel
Snow, Ebenezer
Smith, Joshua
Smith, Jonathan
Smith, John
Simons, Elijah
Squire, David
Stevens, David
Short, John
Sutton, John
Smith, Joshua
Schafer, Peter
Smith, John,
Sebasta, Antonio
Stoddard, Noah
Spooner, Shulab
Seranto, John
Stutson, Smith
Spellman, Elchi
Sterns, John
Seranto, James
Shute, John
Simpson, Charles
Swean, Isaac
Shun, Francis
Skinner, Richard
Stoughton, John
Stanley, W.
Shaver, Archibald
Sullevan, Parks
Stout, Willson
Smith, James
Smith, John
Stout, Willson
Shaw, Thomas
Shaver, Jacob

Shields, William
Sullivan, John
Shadford, William
Seycant, Francis
Smith, Allan
Sailly, Edward
Stearns, John
Spooner, William
Springer, William
Sands, Ewing
Sands, Stephen
Savot, Joseph
Smith, Enoch
Spenser, Solomon
Seabury, Samuel
Stanley, Joseph
Sprage, Jonathan
Shaw, Thomas
Short, John
Simkins, Elias
Seldon, Elias
Stove, Blar
Sanford, Daniel
Stewart, William
Smith, Burwell
Solomon, Ebenezer
Slater, Measr
Smith, Jonathan
Simms, Joshua
Sayers, Cuffe
Sindee, John
Smith, Walter
Southerard, George
Smith, Hugh
Smith, Samuel
Steward, Charles
Stillman, Theodore
Stillman, Ashly
Southard, William
Shepherd, John
Stout, George
Sharp, Philip
Steward, Joseph
Starke, Samuel
Sproat, Thomas
Short, Thomas
Soft, Abraham
Snare, Samuel
Small, Joseph
Simes, James

Slow, Ebenezer
Squibb, Joshua
Stephens, John
Smith, Samuel
Slykes, Richard
Standard, John
Smith, Samuel
Serrea, Sebastin
Seerus, Emanuel
Skelton, John
Southam, Nathaniel
Spalding, Enoch
Sneyders, John
Simons, Samuel
Solley, Nathan
Stevens, Joseph
Serals, Anthony
Simon, William
Simon, James
Samleigh, Pierre
Stilwell, Enoch
Smith, Joshua, 1
Smith, Joshua, 2
Shakly, James
Stafford, Christian
Stewart, Hugh
Steevman, John
Stites, Daniel
Skull, Peter
Seares, Robert
Smith, Jonathan
Stites, Israel
Stuart, Joseph
Stewart, Stephen
Smallwood, Thomas
Smallwood, John
Swaine, Simon
Smith, George
Shuckley, James
Swaine, Zacharius
Shoemaker, Edward
Smith, Jonathan, 2
Sharp, Philip
Shell, Jeremiah
Spur, Nathaniel
Semell, William
Sooper, James
Stratton, Samuel
Saunders, Augustus
Simons, Joseph

Smith, John
Sparefoot, Charles
Smith, Gideon
Scovell, Daniel
Sprywood, Long
Stewart, Edward
Slown, William
Smith, William
Tanner, Casper
Tarena, Townsend
Temare, Jean
Tioffo, Antony
Turk, Joseph
Turner, Thomas
Taber, John
Taber, Thomas
Turner, Thomas
Tripp, Thomas
Thornhill, James
Tillen, Andrew
Taylor, William
Thomas, Abner
Thomas, John
Trop, Jabez
Tabor, John
Thompson, Isaac
Twine, Charles
Thompson, John
Thompson, John
Townsend, Elwell
Thompson, Laurence
Tovell, Francis
Terry, Samuel
Traverse, Christopher
Tucker, Solomon
Tubbs, Saphn
Tebard, Thomas
Tour, Dominick
Thelston, John
Tankason, John
Trout, William
Thomas, Edward
Trendley, William
Trunks, William
Treby, James
Townley, James
Turrine, Peter
Tuden, George
Taylor, Joseph
Tracy, Jessee

Terrett, Thomas
Todd, William
Taylor, Robert
Trailey, Jacob
Thomas, John
Turpin, Lisby
Thaxter, Laban
Tucker, Nathaniel
Tompson, Thomas
Tinleys, Joseph
Thornton, Christian
Tamer, John
Tully, Charles
Tobin, Thomas
Tollings, Francis
Toy, Thomas
Tummer, Gasper
Tucker, Joseph
Thomas, Thomas
Tillunder, Peter
Thompson, Andrew
Tinley, William
Taylor, Tobias
Tripp, Thomas
Twogood, Joseph
Taylor, John
Townsend, William
Trask, Nathaniel
Thistle, Thurdick
Tirve, Jean
Tompkins, Benjamin
Toulger, Sylvanus
Taylor, John
Trefair, Andrew
Tyerill, Thomas
Trott, John
Taber, John
Taylor, Isaac
Talbert, Ebenezer
Thompson, Abraham
Traveno, Richard
Tredwell, James
Turner, Thomas
Trustin, Robert
Thomas, John
Taylor, Robert
Thompson, Seth
Thompson, Robert
Turner, William
Taylor, Alexander

Thomas, John	Taylor, Thomas	Trevett, Edward
Thompson, William	Tiffman, Harvey	Teppett, Henry
Tissina, Stephen	Tapley, Samuel	Turner, George
Tanner, John	Turk, Elias	Thomas, Jean Suplis
Tarrant, John	Trask, Nathaniel	Turpin, Lisby
Tappin, Isaac	Thomas, William	Thompson, William
Talbot, Silas	Tyrant, Jean	Taylor, John
Towns, Samuel	Timcent, Grale	Taylor, Andrew
Tindell, Alexander	Tryan, Edward	Troth, John
Thomas, John	Turner, Thomas	Taylor, Jacob
Tarret, Lewis	Trenchard, Thomas	Thaxter, Seren
Thomas, John	Tillinghost, Thomas	Taylor, Joseph
Townhend, Samuel	Trowbridge, David	Thompson, John
Touzin, Dominica	Tilson, Nicholas	Taylor, John, Captain
Thomas, Green	Table, Samuel	Thompson, Joseph
Turner, John	Turner, John, 1	Tinker, James
Tucker, Robert	Turner, John, 2	Taylor, John
Talbot, Ebenezer	Taylor, John	Tucker, John
Thompson, John	Trusty, George	Trevor, John
Thompson, George	Timford, George	Tobin, James
Twyne, Andrew	Trow, John	Trevo, Job
Taylor, Elias	Townsend, Jacob	Thomas, Joseph
Taylor, Stephen	Taylor, Noadiah	Taylor, John
Tyse, John	Too, Henry	Thurley, Sedon
Twoomey, Dailey	Toppin, Rufus	Teather, George
Thorian, John	Towbridge, Joseph	Turner, Casper
Tucker, Nathan	Thomas, Jessee	Tabee, Anthony
Trivet, Ebenezer	Twigg, Daniel	Taylor, Robert
Turner, William	Tompkins, William	Thomas, John
Taylor, Major	Taylor, Isaac	Tripp, Richard
Terry, William	Tennant, Gilbert	Tavender, Edward
Talbot, Ebenezer	Thompson, Andrew	Trowbridge, Thomas
Terrine, Govenie	Thomas, Cornelius	Torpin, Christopher
Thomas, John	Thompson, Seth	Tally, Archibald
Thorpe, William	Thomas, John	Thandeck, Freeborn
Tucker, Joseph	Tramp, Thomas	Toulger, Robert
Thornton, Christopher	Trescott, Thomas W.	Thomas, Jaques
Tripps, Jacob	Tucker, Seth	Thomas, Ebenezer
Taybor, Samuel	Tilson, John	Tauzin, Domigo
Tippen, Samuel	Taylor, John	Tomay, Thomas
Tucker, John	Taylor, Andrew	Talketon, James
Thompson, John	Thompson, Benjamin	Thompson, William
Turner, Francis	Tevnal, Noah	Tournie, Jean
Tarbour, Antonia	Tenny, Thomas	Threwilt, Gideon
Turner, Caleb	Turner, James	Tryon, Moses
Thompson, Charles	Tucker, Robert	Tosa, Michael
Thompson, William	Thomas, Andrew	Thompson, Joseph
Tucker, John	Teller, John	Taunam, John
Tibbett, Richard	Tantis, Thomas	Tooms, Andrew
Talbott, Ebenezer	Thomas, ——	Trowbridge, Stephen

Thaxter, Lewis
Titcomb, Moses
Thorne, Ebenezer
Taether, Eyah
Tucker, Francis
Titcomb, Michael
Treen, William
Trittou, John
Tolley, Thomas
Truck, Peter
Thomas, Jesse
Tutten, John
Thercy, Robert
Tichett, Henry
Tubby, Thomas
Taylor, Jacob
Tibbards, Samuel
Townsend, Jeremiah
Thompson, William
Thompson, John
Trust, Joseph
Terry, John
Thomas, Urias
Traine, William
Toulean, Piere
Tuck, John
Tessier, Jean
Taylor, John
Thomas, Herod
Towin, John
Thimazun, Simon
Tunkard, Charles
Tabor, Palack
Tillen, Jacob
Thompson, Harvey
Terrett, William
Tilmouse, David
Thornton, Jessee
Tucker, John
Taylor, Gabriel
Tibbs, George
Tollmott, Henry
Turner, Philip
Ternewe, Joshua
Temver, Philip
Templing, John
Talbert, George
Taylor, Jacob
Tucker, Paul
Talbut, William

Thompson, Robert
Thompson, William
Taylor, John
Torrent, Francis
Tomkins, James
Tant, William
Thurston, Benjamin
Truck, Joseph
Thomas, Ebenezer
Thompson, Bartholomew
Tomped, Charles
Tesbard, Zurlen
Towrande, Jille
Turad, Charles
Thomas, James
Taylor, Peter
Thompson, Patrick
Talbert, George
Thornton, Samuel
Thompson, Andrew
Taylor, William
Tresemas, Andric
Tobin, Thomas
Tracy, Nathaniel
Treat, Solomon
Thurston, Samuel
Thomas, Jaque
Taylor, William
Thompson, Israel
Thompson, Robert
Thorner, William
Towser, James
Tracy, Benjamin
Todd, John
Thompson, John
Trowbridge, Benjamin
Totton, Daniel
Thornton, Thomas
Tabowl, Ebenezer
Taylor, Hezekiah
Timrer, Jeremiah
Target, Edward
Uptow, Obadiah
Usher, John
Ullaby, Urson
Union, Joseph
Utinett, Andre
Uuncer, Abimilu
Uncers, Benjamin
Umthank, Thomas

Vallance, George
Verdela, Joseph
Van Dike, Elezier
Vaugh, Richard
Vossery, George
Van Horn, Nathaniel
Vitewell, Joseph
Valentine, Joseph
Vixcane, Juan Albert
Vincent, John
Vinane, Peter
Vigo, Jean
Vin, Lange
Viauf, Jean
Velow, David
Valpey, John
Van Orse, Jean
Van Horn, William
Vestinne, Justin
Vell, David
Vettelet, Pierre
Vaughan, Christian
Vegier, Toser
Velis, Bruno
Vial, John
Venebel, William
Ventis, Moses
Ventis, Samuel
Vandon, Patrick
Verua, Julien
Vibert, William
Vincent, Francis
Veale, Elisha
Vincey, Pattin
Vandross, John
Vanostor, James
Viers, Daniel
Vance, William
Vaughan, Aaron
Vance, William
Vinnal, William
Voss, Henry
Vic, Anare
Vonkett, John
Victory, Roger
Vilvee, John
Vaughan, Andrew
Vingard, Charles
Voe, John
Vann, Christian

Veall, David
Vamp, Nathan
Van Dyke, John
Vasse, Patrick
Vaidel, Peter
Vallet, David
Valem, Piere
Vissenbouf, Jean
Vessoco, Peter
Vandegrest, Francis
Viegra, David
Varley, Barnabus
Vitena, Andrew
Virnon, Robert
Vorus, John
Vandergrest, Thomas
Vierse, William
Von Won, William
Vickery, John
Vallett, John
Vallett, Antonio
Vookly, Nicholas
Ward, Charles
Waterman, Thomas
Waterman, William
Walsey, John
Warley, Joseph
Wyatt, Benjamin
Wellis, John
Wilcox, Edward
Wilson, Benjamin
Wimondesola, Vincent
Walker, Michael
West, Jabez
Waistcoat, Ezekiel
Williams, Barley
Wilts, George
Wells, Ezra
Whitney, James
Walker, Samuel
Wright, Nathaniel
Williams, Samuel
Williams, Isaac
White, William
Weatherall, Jacob
Walters, Roger
Wyley, Henry
Wilderidger, Robert
Willson, Francis
Willson, Thomas

Welch, Mathew
Wyer, William
Waymore, Andrew
Williams, Amos
Willis, John
Waldrick, John
Waters, Thomas
Williams, Edward
Warsell, Thomas
Wolf, John
Wessells, John
White, Samuel
Williams, Jonathan
Williams, James
Wood, Mathew
Whipple, Christian
Warrinham, Richard
Williamson, William
Wells, Cornelius
Walley, Joseph
Wilson, William
Warn, William Taylor
White, Watson
Williams, Charles
Willis, Abel
Willis, Frederick
Waterman, Asariah
Winnemore, Jacob
Waistcoat, Charles
Wilcox, Obadiah
Whipple, Benjamin
Waterman, Asher
Waterman, William
Willeman, John
Wheaton, Jesse
Whitlock, John
Wessell, William
Wood, George
Wells, Gideon
Wyatt, William
White, Sampson
Watson, Robert
Weatherox, Joseph
Willoson, Guy
Watson, Edward
Williams, Moses
Walker, Richard
Wormner, Cornelius
Witham, Thomas
Willis, Joseph

Welch, Robert
Williams, George
Wright, John
Woop, James
Wenthoff, Joseph . /
Watts, John
Williams, James
Wallis, Anthony
Walpole, Robert
Williams, John
White, Benjamin
Walker, Nathaniel
Walker, Thomas
Ward, Joseph
Wilcox, Isaac
Wyatt, Stamford
Walker, David
Wood, Daniel
Williams, James
Webb, Jacob
Woodward, Joseph
Wing, Stephen
Wakefield, Joseph
Wilmarth, Samuel
White, John
White, John
Woodman, Nathaniel
Warner, Amos
White, Samuel
Wessell, Joseph
Williams, Nicholos
Ward, Thomas
Weeks, Lemuel
Walton, Jonathan
Wimondesolo, Vincent
Wales, Samuel
Wales, Ephraim
Webb, James
Winter, Stephen
Waller, Caleb
Willian, John Foster
Williams, John
Williams, Henry
Williams, John
White, John
White Thomas
Wood, Charles
Walmer, William
Wells, Richard
Wright, John

Wilson, Benjamin
Wier, John
Wright, Robert
Wimensold, Vincent
Waddle, Christian
Weeks, Francis
Wright, John
Williams, Dodd
Walker, Nathaniel
Wood, Charles
Wright, John
Willson, Benjamin
Willson, James
Williams, Jonathan
Wilcox, Edward
Walker, Thomas
Wattles, Henry
Wheeler, Michael
Warren, Jonathan
Wedden, William
Wessell, Joseph
White, Benjamin
Wood, Charles
Whitlock, Joseph
Wheeler, Morrison
West, Richard
Williams, Cato
Wood, Lachwal
Williams, John
Wilkins, Charles
Webb, James
Whetton, Jesse
Whitehead, Jacob
Whittemore, Jacob
Warner, Samuel, 1
Warner, Samuel, 2
Wheeler, William
Wire, David
Wharton, Loyd
Wubberd, William
Wandall, John
Walden, Asa
White, Ichabod
Williams, Ephraim
Williams, John
Whipple, Benjamin
Wheeler, Joseph
Williams, Stephen
Woesin, John
Williams, Samuel

Wallace, Joseph
Wallis, Ezekiel
Williams, Thomas
Williams, Charles
White, Robert
Woodward, Rosen
Wallis, John
Willor, Abraham
Wiglott, Micheal
Welanck, John
Watson, Henry
Witherton, Soloman
White, Richard
Woist, Henry
Woodley, Henry
Willis, William
Woodward, Thomas
Wood, Daniel
Waistcoat, Jacob
Waters, Henry
Wood, Daniel
Watson, John, 2
Wood, Edward
Wells, William
Williams, John
William, John
William, Joseph
Walker, Michael
Wolf, Henry
Whitlock, William
Wadler, Christopher
West, Edward
Willshe, Benjamin
Woodman, David
Williams, Jonathan
Whelton, John
Walcott, Joseph
Whiteman, Harman
Wellman, Mathew
White, John
Watson, Robert
Whellan, Michael
Whithousen, Cardway
Williams, Isaac
Wheeler, William
Williams, Peter
Whitney, George
Whiting, George
Wolf, Henry
Willson, George

Williamson, William
Wannell, Ezekiel
Williams, John
Warner, John
Wilson, James
Watson, Robert
Wall, James
Watson, William
Warde, John
Willeroon, Benjamin
Whellen, James
Waitscoat, Jabez
West, Jabez
Witherly, John
Woomstead, Michael
Warf, William
Welch, James
Walton, John
Wilkinson, William
West, Jabez
Wendell, Isaac
Windser, Joseph
Watson, John
Welk, Nellum
Warrell, Christopher
Warton, Loyd
Williams, Richard
Walker, Samuel
Wibert, Felix
Warnock, Robert
Wanton, George
Wittle W.
White, John
Whitmolk, Samuel
Whitemore, Luther
Willson, John
Webb, Thomas
Ward, Willlam
Wellman, Timothy
Walter, John
Webb, Oliver
Warren, Benjamin
Willson, John
Warrin, Obadiah
Widgon, Learen
Warner, Obediah
Walter, George
Winn, Samuel
Wade, Benjamin
Wade, Thomas

Waterman, John
Willard, Julian
Willard, John
Wilson, Nathaniel
Waterman, Calvin
Webb, William
White, Thomas
Willard, George
Watt, John
Wood, Champion
Waiterly, Joseph
Webb, Thomas
Whiting, James
White, William
Waistcoat, Jacob
Wood, Daniel
Willson, W.
Woodley, Henry
Whitepair, William
Welch, James
Webb, Jonathan
Wright, John
Williams, Henry
Watkins, Thomas
Westward, Philip
Wen, Patrick
Whila, John
Wilson, Patrick
Wilson, John
Webb, John
Welch, James
Wells, Peter
Woodfall, Thomas
Wanstead, Michael
Webber, William
Wood, Joseph
Whethase, Horatio
Wood, John
Whiting, William
Whiting, George
Wallis, Hugh
Webber, William
Welch, Isaac
Welch, James
Whiting, George
Woodley, Henry
Welch, Moses
Wood, Justus
Watkins, Thomas
Wright, Charles

Witless, William
Webb, Nathaniel
Walton, Henry
Wigglesworth, John
Wilkinson, Amos
Watkins, Thomas
Williams, Benjamin
Winngman, Jacob
Wattle, William
Woodbury, Herbert
Woodbury, Luke
Woodbury, Jacob
Walker, Michael
Watkins, Thomas
Wallis, Jonathan
Wigman, Stephen
Willson, John
Wilcox, Pardon
Wilcox, Edward
Washington, Townsend
Walker, George
Weeks, Francis
Whitney, Peter
White, Sampson
Watson, Thomas
Wood, Jonathan
Wickery, Conrad
Waterman, Asher
Willson, William
White, Ephern
Williston, Abraham
Waterman, Samuel
Walker, John
Wright, John
Ward, Benjamin
Wansley, Powers A
Warmsley, Joseph
Winters, Joseph
Whipple, Samuel
Whipple, Stephen
Wheeler, Henry
White, Lemuel
Woodly, Ralph
Wallesly, George
Wooten, William
Wallis, James
Wainscott, Mathew
Whater, Michael
Watson, Henry
Walker, Nathaniel

Wells, William
White, Joseph
Wigley, William
White, William
Weaver, Thomas
Warne, Christopher
Wedon, David
Wier, John
Weston, Simon
Warner, Thomas
Walker, William
Wareman, Elijah
Walls, Edward
White, William
Walker, Baldwin
Weeks, James
Winslow, Seth
Wallis, Benjamin
Wharfe, John
White, John
Webb, Michael
Wise, John
Windgate, Edward
Wood, William
Wainwright, Joseph
Warky, Unct
Webb, William
Williams, George
Wallis, George
Wind, Gilleam
Warrington, William
Wedger, John
Willet, James
Wigmore, John
Wetherby, Jesse
Willin, Day
Wester, Samuel
Wood, Jabez
Wallsey, William
Wood, Joseph
Williams, William
West, Richard
Walters, Jonathan
Wartridge, Joseph
Woolock, Michael
Williams, John
Welsh, John
Welsh, David
Walker, William
Watson, Thomas

61

Williams, John
Williams, Nathaniel
Wardling, James
Winter, George
Walter, Joseph
Wilson, Edward
Whitehouse, Enoch
Webster, Francis
Waggstaff, Richard
Wade, Thomas
Warner, Andrew
Webby, George
Wood, Samuel
Walker, Daniel
Walding, George
Willson, Timothy
Whitney, Isaac
Williams, James
Webb, John
Williams, John
Watson, Thomas
Watts, Joseph
Webber, Joseph
Whitney, John
Wallace, Bartholomew
Wallace, John
Wallar, Ebenezer
Wallore, John
Wallace, Thomas
Williams, Jeffrey
Welpley, Joseph
Woody, Edward
Woodhull, David
Wyatt, John
Weston, William
Worthy, James
Warner, Berry
Ward, Simon
Williman, John
Woodworth, Abel
Watson, John
Wells, Joseph
Webb, John
Wyax, Gordon
Ward, Christenton

Waterman, William
Wardell, Benjamin
Walker, Joseph
Watts, Samuel
Watts, Thomas
Woody, John
Ward, David
Willson, Martin
Willis, John
Waistcot, John
Williams, Ethkin
Weekman, William
Watson, John
Whippley, Christopher
White, James
Wentworth, Robert
Willis, Joseph
Willman, Joseph
Watkins, John
Wear, James
West, Benjamin
Whittaker, Joseph
Wickward, Samuel
Weston, Henry
Wickman, Joseph
White, Timothy
Whade, Thomas
Wheaton, Joseph
Woodbury, William
Woodbury, Robert
Woodbury, Nathaniel
Weeks, Thomas
Woodwell, Gideon
Williams, William
Wilson, Lawrence
Watson, Nathaniel
Walker, Ezekiel
Welch, Philip
Withpane, William
Waters, John
Winter, Charles
Wainscott, Jacob
Welch, Ezekiel
Woodson, James
Williams, George
Withington, Robert

Welch, George
Willhouse, Conway
Whelan, Michael
Wilmot, Luke
Weeks, Seth
Wright, Joseph
Walker, Michael
Wardell, John
Wellman, John
Wyatt, John
Watson, Joseph
Wyckoff, Reuben
Walker, Hezekiah
Walsh, Patrick
Xmens, John
Young, Alexander
Yorke, Edward
Younger, Louis
Young, John
Yduchare, Francis
Young, Daniel
Yanger, Joseph
Young, Archibald
Young, George
Young, William
Young, Jacob
Yard, Joseph
Young, Charles
Youngans, Charles
Yose, Peter
Young, Marquis
Yoannett, George
York, Edward
Young, Seth
Young, Ichabod
Yeager, Adam
Young, Marquis
Yeaston, Jacob
Yedrab, Pender
Yates, Thomas
Young, John
Yalkington, Joseph
Yeason, Jacob
Zuran, Piere
Zamiel, Jean Peter

www.ingramcontent.com/pod-product-compliance
Lightning Source LLC
Chambersburg PA
CBHW021526090426

42739CB00007B/794